THIS WORLD AND THAT

An Analysis of Psychic Communications

I it possible to have genuine communication between the livin the dead and what are the obstacles which stand in the way p we find some rational explanation for the phenomena of s and the seance room These are some of the question essed in this book, written by a British psychiatrist, Dr. L. J. ht, and his wife, Phoebe P. yne, a natural clairvoyant. He al experience and his medical training uniquely qualified consider together these and ther subjects, viewing the at ntext of m s nature d apacities. N pat answers but rather tenders couraged to think for himself about mysterious age the world and the next.

Not only hav authors estion of survival after the death o e body, ey hed on the wider implications of the chic su g between its positive and negative and in connection with medical diag other ways. This book is an analysis sm from the viewpoint everyday life

THIS WORLD AND THAT

An Analytical Study
of
Psychic Communication

by
PHOEBE D. PAYNE
(Mrs. L. J. Bendit)
and
LAURENCE J. BENDIT, M.A., M.D. (Cantab.)

A QUEST BOOK
Published under a grant from The Kern Foundation

THE THEOSOPHICAL PUBLISHING HOUSE
Wheaton, Ill., U.S.A.
Madras, India / London, England

To

KENNETH RICHMOND

and other Co-Workers

FOREWORD TO QUEST BOOK EDITION

This book, originally published in Britain in 1950, seems still to hold its validity after a good many years. It has been criticized by some for leaving so much open and for not being sufficiently dogmatic to please those who like their information in sealed packages, rather than trying to find their own true answers. This, however, seems to be one of the virtues of the book. If it makes one think, it has accomplished its task, for the reader is much more likely to find enduring satisfaction that way, rather than from being taught, as in a kindergarten. In any case, in a subject such as the link between the psychic and the dense physical world, questions and doubts can and should arise.

Since the original publication, one of the writers, having passed into the next world, has now direct experience of what, when this book was written, had still to be filtered through the brain. It would be interesting to know how much she would now want to revise this text. I suspect, not very much, if only because of the doors left open in it. One day we shall all know for ourselves: which is something to hope for, not to fear.

L.J.B.

CONTENTS

PERSONAL FOREWORDS

I

The purpose of this book is to set out certain aspects of my personal experience and to explain it. Consequently, it may not be irrelevant if it is prefaced by a certain amount of autobiographical material, as this will help to make clear how it came to be written in this form.

To be born clairvoyant is an odd thing, because one is quite unable to assess ordinary life without its counterpart of extra-sensory perception. I do not remember a time when the visible world did not play into or through another world. For a long time I had no idea where one ended and the other began: they were both to me ordinary and natural, and they belonged together.

As a small and isolated child I did not realise my loneliness because there were always such a lot of interesting things to observe. True, life was often confusing and frightening. Some people behaved unaccountably, while others were far easier to understand in that they made no sudden demands upon one. But it took some time before I was able to sort out consciously any kind of difference between my subjective and objective worlds.

In this way, life has always had a double texture. The world of the living and of ordinary affairs wove itself across the pattern of the so-called dead and their environment. It was therefore logical enough that, as a child, I should find it extremely difficult to understand what people meant by death, or why they were gloomy about the subject. Perhaps I can best illustrate my meaning by describing what happened when I was about ten years old. It was my first experience of death in the family. My great-grandmother had a sudden heart attack while I was having tea with her, and though I ran for help, she died almost at once. Everyone was prepared for grief on my part, because I was passionately devoted to her and preferred to be with her rather than with anyone else. To their astonishment, I went on quite serenely and happily until the time of the funeral, when my parents left me at home in charge of a maid. I went upstairs to watch the cortège start. It seemed strange to me that so much fuss was made about a coffin, that there should be flowers and black clothes. But grown-up people did odd things, anyway, so I made no comment. When the procession slowly moved off, I could bear this stupidity no longer. I flung up the window and leaned out, calling, 'You silly people. Where are you going? Grannie is here with *me*!' To my perception that was completely true: Grannie stood by my side, looking very natural but rather more radiant than usual. Failing to make any impression on the disappearing funeral cortège, I shut the window and had a long talk with the old lady. She explained that she had gladly left a tired and old physical body; that she now felt strong and well; and that she could do many of the things she had hoped to do for years past. The conversation was quite ordinary, but full of the zest and interest with which I was familiar.

The family were surprised at my unconcerned attitude about our loss, but murmured that children easily forget. This was, however, not true. To me, there was no sense of loss nor any cause for grief. In my own way I felt in close touch with my grandmother; she was alive, so what was there to worry about? And ever since, life after death has been to me a natural and sequential part of human experience.

Later, as I developed, death naturally presented many questions to my mind and threw up problems which I am still in the process of solving. But being accustomed to the presence of dead people is only a small part of the psychic's life, the threads of which naturally weave themselves through the commonplace happenings of everyday life.

As is usual with the child who is psychic from birth, I did not talk of this other world, or realise that my perception of life was different from that of other people. It was muddling and it bothered me a great deal. There was, for instance, the question of good manners and courtesy. Why, for instance, was it polite to greet people who entered the house by the front door, while others who arrived, perhaps through the wall, were entirely ignored?

All this, and many similar things made a surprisingly difficult childhood. Later, in my teens, when I awoke with a bad shock to the fact that I was unusual in this respect, I immediately began to seek for the reasons for this difference. From that moment until now, I have been searching for the laws which govern the psychic life and its phenomena.

My first book, *Man's Latent Powers*, was an attempt to make my experience objective, and to give some reasons, as far as I had then discovered them, for some of these many problems.

I have never, at any time, been a spiritualist, but I have worked among them for years. I have sat in hundreds of séances, always carefully observing and making mental notes, always knowing there were a number of alternative reasons for the output in these séances. I realised more strongly as time went on that psychological knowledge was imperative if one were to find one's way through the maze of difficulties which mediumship and psychic phenomena present to a clear-minded person.

I eventually underwent a personal analysis, sifting out my obvious psychological problems from my dual psychic experience and learning to classify and to set the perceptions due to psychic perceptivity side by side with the ordinary mental and emotional tangles of my life. All this personal work threw a flood of light on the psychic field. I saw the muddle of the séance room in quite a new way, and I began to observe not only with my psychic perception but also with new psychological insight.

My own therapeutic work, too, took on new values. I continued to study not only psychology but the philosophy of the vast realm of symbolism, simple physics and chemistry, and the wide field of electro-magnetic radiation. Then, when I married, I pooled whatever specialised knowledge I had with my husband and together we wrote *The Psychic Sense*.

The present book is a continuation of our experience. If, in some ways, I seem to contradict some of the things I wrote in my first book, it is not really so. It is that I have travelled on and now see things in a new light.

My constant work with the casualties of unwise psychic development has shown me many things about the human being and his make up, in which his unconscious mind, as well as his conscious field, each play an important part, especially in regard to psychism.

Nevertheless, we are all beginners in this science, and we do not know the answers to our problems. We are only groping our way towards them. This means that, having seen a partial truth, we often have to relinquish it in order to reach out toward a further development of that truth.

As to myself, I can only say that I am this kind of person, this has been my experience; and if there is truth and value in *any* kind of experience, then this is as true to me as some totally different outlook on life would be to another person. One may be amused, angry, or try to dismiss altogether this difficult yet common subject, but I believe that every human being is endowed with his own quality of psychic perceptivity, and a mechanism which may or may not consciously respond to his experience. The universe has endless potentialities, witness the amazing progress of science during the last few years. Man himself has the same potentialities, and is slowly extending his use of the human senses so that he may become increasingly conscious of these possibilities, both within himself and in the world outside.

When our latent powers become integrated with the conscious field and we have control over our own faculties, then the many avenues of their use in art, science, education and therapy will be immeasurably increased, and they will acquire an intrinsic beauty which is as yet far from us.

This book is bound to be faulty, but it has at least the merit that it is a sincere attempt to express a little more objectively an aspect of life which is entirely natural, and without which I personally should have no experience of any kind.

P.D.P.

II

This is the third book which I have been concerned with writing, and which has to do with *Psi*. *Psi* is the term given to-day in scientific circles to the mental function by which paranormal cognition, also called paracognition, extra-sensory perception, clairvoyance, telepathy and all forms of 'psychism' takes place. Three books on one small aspect of the vast field of human psychology seem a lot, yet there has been a reason for each of them. The first, *The Psychic Sense*, was, like this one, written in collaboration with my wife. It was a first attempt to bring together psychological knowledge and the results of her experience of 'psychic' matters. Further, from a personal point of view it was an experiment, not to say a piece of research for both of us. My wife tells me that she clarified a great deal of what she knew about psychology, while I learned a lot about psychism. When the book was published, moreover, we had some amusement at our friends' expense when they tried to disentangle the parts which each of us had specifically written: they usually reversed things, and attributed to me what my wife had expounded, while giving her the parts which had come from my own pen.

There was a need for this book in that the majority of psychologists did not recognise or understand *psi* as being what it is: a thing which, quite apart from any subjective psychological problems, can cause confusion and difficulty to their patients. Paracognition is perception of things *outside* one's own mind, and existing in their own right. This is a very different matter from cognising the products of that mind itself, and projected from *inside* it into the field of consciousness. To see a real, live ghost is one thing; to be aware of a dream or a self-created vision is another, and nobody had previously tried to explain the difference.

The second book, *Paranormal Cognition*, was merely a rider to the first. It was a slightly emended reprint of a thesis sent to Cambridge University where it was accepted

Personal Forewords

for my degree of Doctor of Medicine. It was a clinical study, and it was presented in a form more suited to the academic mind than was *The Psychic Sense*. Apart from raising some philosophical considerations, however, it added nothing to the ground already covered by the earlier book.

This third volume is thus really a successor to the first. In our opinion it needs writing in order to amplify the general principles already stated, by going into a number of specific subjects concerned with *psi* and allied phenomena, and trying to get them into some sort of focus. This can only be achieved by making use of the knowledge which the relatively modern science of psychology has given us. For, new as it is—in the West, at least—it contains a great deal which is of value in a study such as this, and without it we are left still very much in the dark.

In the first part of this preface, my wife has outlined how she has reached her present position. My own approach has been from a totally different angle, in that I came to it as a result of my training as a medical psychologist or psychiatrist, by a series of logical steps derived from my own experience.

When I decided to forsake general practice in favour of this branch of medicine, I determined to undergo what is technically called a 'training analysis'. This is rightly held by many to be an essential for anybody who wants to do more than the most superficial form of psychotherapy. The trainee puts himself in the position of a patient and undergoes a course of psychological analysis. By so doing, not only is he expected to learn to know himself, but he also learns, by the only possible means, to understand for himself the problems of his patients, and how to deal with them. As I was never more than a half-hearted believer in

17

Freudian doctrines, I went to an analyst who, though not accepting the psycho-analytical dogma, worked on 're-ductive' lines: that is, he made me go back and back through my adolescence and the experiences of childhood until I eventually recalled what may have been actual memories of infancy and even of intra-uterine life. It was most interesting and I learned a great deal from the process. Moreover, it did something towards removing various personal difficulties and tangles from my character. But at the end of the analysis I was still unsatisfied.

The next stage began when I heard Professor C. G. Jung speak. I realised that here was another key to the problems of life, and I set to work to study on his lines and found that, because of his appreciation of the spiritual factor, he took me a long way further than I had hitherto reached. Jung has done a great work: he has linked science and religion and has shown that in the psychological sphere there is no conflict possible between true science and true religion. The operative word is 'true'. The only trouble is that he does not go far enough and that certain aspects of experience are not clearly mapped out in his study but remain blank even though their existence is appreciated.

During this period I also heard Professor William Mc-Dougall speak of the work of Dr. J. B. Rhine and give his opinion of it with characteristic balance: he said, in effect, 'I never believe anything absolutely. But I think that Rhine has proved beyond reasonable doubt that extra-sensory perception'—the term *psi* had not then been coined—'is a scientific fact'. This was my first intimation that laboratory work had actually proved the existence of 'psychic' powers.

A little later I first made personal contact with my wife. I had for some years met her in groups and discussions and

18

had always respected her as a psychic, if only because, unlike many of her kind, she was willing to listen to and
consider the opinions of those who did not agree with her.
Moreover, she would often say, 'I don't know': another
phenomenon rare among professed psychics. At this point,
however, I began to work more closely with her and discovered that the only real answer to a good many problems
which analysis, both reductive and on the lines of Jung,
had left unresolved, lay in a realisation that *psi* was at the
back of them. Many of my troubles, both as a child and in
later life, were due to my being sufficiently paracognitive,
without realising it, to get myself into bad psychic tangles
which no amount of subjective analysis could undo.

One of the things I found, as a result of this 'placing', or
integrating of my own *psi* function with my conscious
mind, was that, whereas in the first state I was constantly
being caught out by it and receiving shocks in my 'solar
plexus', I gradually became aware of its activity in a different way. It was as if the centre of its action were no longer
in the pit of the stomach but in the middle of my head.
Further, whereas in the first stage it had something of a
tactile or at least sensory quality, causing subjective sensations in that part of my body, in the latter, it became
something which I can only describe as 'pure cognition' or
'unconditioned awareness'. In the unintegrated phase there
was no clarity in what I perceived, and I was likely to
react or to be myself in some way emotionally moved,
either towards or away from the object or person causing
the reaction, so that there was always a danger of psychological identification with the situation. In the positive
phase, however, there is a clear, cold knowledge of what is
happening, but there is no kind of movement in myself.

This does not mean that I—or anybody else I know—

19

always succeed in maintaining this level, but it is obviously the thing to aim at and to be gradually achieved. I have described this experience as one of pure or unconditioned awareness because, in my own case at least, this is how I know things reaching me through *psi*: I am not clairvoyant, or clairaudient, or clairesentient, and I think that these specialised modes of *psi* activity represent a secondary elaboration of the pure perception, which takes place directly in the mind, prior to any translation into the language of any particular sense. This confirms my belief that many writers whose works are rich in metaphors, whether of sight, sound or feeling, are in effect translating what pure mental perception through *psi* has given them, into appropriate imagery in whatever terms suit their immediate purpose. In any case, one thing stands out, which is that proper training of *psi*, as an ancillary to psychological integration, brings about not only a clearer understanding and awareness of things and people, but also relieves one of a great deal of functional stress and even of shock. This may cause difficulties where the digestion or the heart are concerned, and may result in more or less severe and unaccountable headaches.

It is worth adding that this conception of *psi*, in its cognitive aspects, as being a single 'sense' instead of manifesting as a series of mental senses corresponding to the five distinct physical senses, is not in accord with the description given in *The Psychic Sense*. It is, however, the view which we now hold, as a result of further study and development of our ideas.

I learned, further, that this factor was important, not only in myself but in a great many patients of the more sensitive kind, and that it required to be dealt with explicitly and intelligently if they were to be helped more than superficially. This opinion has not changed with the years. But it does not mean that I have thrown over my psychology and become a monomaniac. Both sides need to be taken together and one is as important as the other.

I have, on the other hand, had unusual opportunity of studying the subject of paracognition in daily life. Through close contact with a number of naturally psychic people, I have learned something of their temperament and of the difficulties which beset them in these clamorous, violent days. I have also learned something of both the strength and the limitations of *psi*. It is a source of information, and hence of *knowledge*, but it does not, in itself, bring *wisdom*. To be wise requires a deeper understanding than comes through psychism alone—and, for that matter, from any other avenue through which knowledge is acquired. It needs something which comes from the heart and neither from the head, with its intellect, nor from the 'solar plexus', the seat of much negative psychism and much un-co-ordinated emotionalism. I also realised the confusion which psychism without some degree of wisdom leaves in the minds of its victims.

This book is an attempt to clear up some of that confusion. To some it may seem that it is not sufficiently scientific and takes too much for granted. To others it may appear too much so, and too destructive of comfortable beliefs. That cannot be helped. We have tried to keep an objective, scientific attitude to the subject, and to carry this attitude into realms where the scientific experimental method cannot be applied. But we have not hesitated to go beyond the point to which objectivity can take us, and have expressed something of our own personal beliefs. That we have done this does not weaken our position. Even scientists must be permitted to have beliefs based on inner knowledge and experience, and all that can legitimately be demanded of them in this realm is that they shall be tentative and suggestive, not dogmatic. (True science, in any case, can never be dogmatic: it is only pseudo-science which falls into this error.) So we have tried to avoid didacticism and to leave every question open. It is for the reader to make up his own mind about the answers. Like my wife, I conclude by saying this is my experience: it is valid to me, as far as it goes and I stand by it until life changes my point of view—as indeed it must, if I am not to be numbered among the unburied dead.

L.J.B.

1

WHAT IS MAN?

Before going into the main subject of this book, it is essential that we should have some idea of the central figure in it, man. For although communication between the psychic and the physical world is probably universal throughout nature, it offers no problem except to him. Being what he is, man is incapable of letting natural processes take care of themselves, and he tries to interfere with them and to improve on them. The result is that life becomes for him a complicated matter, full of snares and pitfalls which do not exist for the simple, unself-conscious lower animals. The latter are subjected to forces and impulses which manifest themselves as instinct, and if the animal allows himself to be carried by the tides and currents of Nature, he gets through the routine of his existence without trouble.

Man is different from the animal in that he is self-conscious. The core of his being, and that which makes him other than merely animal, is his sense of identity. He has what Western psychology designates as the ego, more forcefully described in Sanskrit literature as *Ahamkara*, or 'I-am-ness'. The Sanskrit form is a good one because

What is Man?

of its strong assertion that '*I am*'. It suggests the will to go our own way, to do what we choose, the refusal to be vaguely blown about by the winds of circumstance. It suggests also the obstinacy of the person who refuses to learn from others and who, because of this obstinacy, gets into difficulties which a more docile creature would avoid. This is precisely what happens.

Man's egoism is at once his strength and his weakness. It is his weakness because, as Matthias Alexander[1] points out, man, despite his intelligence, does far less well for himself than animals do. He eats the wrong food, his posture is bad, and altogether he is a poor specimen from the viewpoint of physical health. This Alexander attributes to the obscuration of instinctive behaviour by the growth of intelligence. Man has learned a little about nature and tries to run his life self-consciously, in the light of that knowledge. But what he knows is so partial that he constantly makes mistakes and so gets himself into trouble.

On the positive side, egoism gives man his power. For one thing it makes him inquisitive. He wants to know about things. Lower animals may seem to be just as curious but there is always some material purpose behind their quest: food, a mate, or something of practical worth or interest. Man, however, often seeks knowledge for its own sake, that is, for abstract value, and tries to extend that knowledge by every means. He not only uses his physical senses, but he adds to them by means of instruments which reveal to him things he could not observe unaided. He also gathers together data which he correlates and from which he then deduces further information, often of an abstract rather than a concrete nature.

[1] *Man's Supreme Inheritance.*

What is Man?

He realises, too, that the knowledge he acquires enables him to turn things to his own ends by properly directed exertion. If he knows how they work he can use that knowledge to harness and direct them for purposes other than those which they would achieve without his intervention. Falling water, which would merely flow downhill until it reached the sea, is used to turn mills and so save man's energies for other things. Or the same natural source of power can be converted to indirect use so that the electricity it generates lights and heats cities far removed from any river. Without man such things could not happen.

So man is a power and he knows it. But both that power and the knowledge of it are centred round the sense that he himself exists, and hence has a freedom of action and of choice which the lower animal has not.

That self and its power are not, however, gifts which appear in man full-grown. On the contrary, they are prizes which he has to wrest from nature by hard toil on the evolutionary path. For man's body belongs to the animal kingdom. It is motivated by instinct and tends to follow the patterns which instinct imposes. These are, in the main, simple enough. They govern the actions which makes for the preservation of the species: feeding, procreation, self-defence or escape. In their purest form they are undiscriminating and, given certain circumstances, every individual is apt to behave exactly in the same manner as every other member of his species. In the case of solitary animals it shows in behaviour typical of the species or variety as a whole, so that an observer can predict fairly well what it will do under given conditions. In the case of gregarious kinds, individual action is co-ordinated so as to fit in with the pattern of the collective

25

group. Bees and ants, and even the evolutions of a flight of birds, show this very clearly. Instinctive patterns, moreover, are not learned, they are innate. A caged bird which has never been in contact with its kind nevertheless builds a characteristic nest at the same time as all others, whether caged or wild. That is, instinct is both unconscious, in that it does not depend on conscious learning, and it is collective rather than individual in that single animals all tend to follow the same routine under similar general conditions. Further, it does not reach the animal through his physical senses and hence may be thought of as reaching him telepathically, or through a primitive psychic sense.

Man, on the other hand, is characteristically inclined to behave as an individual. The more he asserts himself as man, the more individual his behaviour becomes. He uses his mind to choose his course of action and is often prompted to deny himself the satisfaction of instinct because, for one reason or another, he chooses to do so. A hungry man faced with food would instinctively grab it, but he may hold back from gratifying the instinctive urge either because he wants to do something else before eating, or because he wants to leave the food for others, or because it is not his to take.

Instinct belongs to past evolution: it represents that which the race or species collectively have learned from their early experience. It belongs to the mass rather than to the individual, and its mandates are imposed on the individual unconsciously. Further, it dictates immediate behaviour, in the present, and with no conscious anticipation of the future. This assertion may seem to be denied by the behaviour of animals which lay in stores for the winter, especially when they correctly anticipate that it will be a particularly rigorous one. But it seems unlikely that there is any conscious intelligence in the squirrel which makes him think out his needs in advance. He does so, most likely, because blind instinct drives him to do so in the present moment, and he carries out his orders despite the fact that he may be in a zoo where such stores will be quite superfluous. In the same way, it appears that the sexual instinct demands immediate action, without anticipation of its results—a fact only too often and too painfully realised even where human beings are concerned. It is only as physiological changes take place that the sexual pattern changes to the parental and that preparations are made for the young to be born.

In short, man at this stage is in a state where conflicting forces are at work. He is animal in that he has an animal body in which the primitive urges of instinct are active, but there are other forces also which often pull against them and sometimes inhibit them altogether. He does this because of his power of abstract thought, his sense that the immediate present is connected with times and places more remote, and beyond the range of his concrete senses. Hence, as his mentality grows, he learns that there are times when immediate satisfaction of impulse may imperil his success in achieving aims which are ultimately more important than the immediate pleasure of self-gratification.

We may put it that instinct emerges from the past and makes its impact on the present. But in man the future also calls: that is, anticipation of things which can and will be achieved and which are different from those which have been done in the past. There is also a more or less blind groping towards some goal of achievement and success which the individual sets before himself. As man grows, so does the relative importance of this motive grow and affect his life more profoundly. He is no longer

What is Man?

content to satisfy his immediate desires, he tries to harness and adapt these desires to his future—or, in the jargon, teleological—aims.

It is, so to speak, at the point where these two forces meet, the instinctive out of the past, the teleological out of the future, that the ego comes into manifestation, that man's consciousness of himself, is focused. Here it is born and grows as intellect develops, widening the field over which it has control; reaching back into the past as memory, into the future as anticipation. It overlaps onto the realm of instinct on the one hand and onto that of teleological urges on the other, and it is ever striving to synthesise the two into a harmonious whole, and so to reach happiness.

In this way we have a picture of man as a triple being. There is his animal nature: the body and its instinctive urges on one side; the ego and its mental field in the centre; and a mysterious third factor, implicit rather than explicit, drawing him forward into futurity on the other side. This latter we may, for the sake of simplicity, call spirit, while we can identify the soul with the mind of psyche: a thing traditionally held to be different from spirit or *pneuma*, but nowadays only too often confused with it.

This scheme, which is in line with St. Paul and the Neo-Platonists gives us a blue-print of man. But it is more than a theory, for we can to some extent verify it for ourselves by examining our subjective experience. The conflict between selfish gratification of instinct and the suppression or control of desire because of expediency, shows us something of our own make-up. Very often, also, we can recognise the ego as that part of us which recognises the conflict and feels the double pull. There are, however, other and more elaborate ways of seeing the

28

same thing and thereby seeing it more in detail. Perhaps the most common is our experience of time, which we know in three phases, each of which corresponds to one of the three divisions of man enumerated above.

Let us first consider that such study must of necessity be made from the viewpoint of the ego: it is 'I' who am examining these things. But I can only do so if I think and feel about them; that is, I must use my mind or soul just as I should use hands or eyes to examine material objects about me. From that standpoint I can recognise my body. It has its own level of life, its own sensations, its own power of action. Moreover, much of its life takes place, whether I like it or not, in tune with certain rhythms and phases of time. It likes to wake, eat, sleep, in more or less regular patterns. The heart, the breath, the menstrual cycle and many other activities of the body follow the track of that form of time which exists in the physical world, and I cannot do a great deal about it. True, my state of mind—or soul—can affect physical function to some extent. But if my state of mental excitement or tension is relieved, the body tends to fall back into its normal rhythm. The body, in short, is that part of my being which is ruled by time. But that time is not my own, it exists outside me and holds sway over the objective, material world just as it does over my own body. We will, for the sake of clarity, qualify it and call it *absolute, physical,* or *earth time.*

The qualification is needed because I do not know this time directly with my mind. To keep myself in tune with it I have to consult instruments which tell me where I am with regard to it. So my conscious and willed activity at the physical level is adapted to an artificial measure of absolute time which I register by looking at my clock.

What is Man?

The reason I do not know absolute time is that the time in which my mental processes take place is different. It is measured against no physical standard but depends on my mood, my 'state of mind'. If I am interested, a period of absolute time goes quickly, if bored, it drags slowly past. In short, mental time is elastic and plastic, and mental processes can take place in it so quickly that they appear to be out of time altogether. They are, however, not so, because even though a mass of data may be shown me at once and seem to be understood simultaneously, careful scrutiny shows that they are only taken in one at a time, no matter how rapidly the mind travels from item to item. The process is akin to that which makes a television picture appear as a whole, whereas in actual fact it is made up by a dot of light moving with incredible speed across and across the fluorescent screen.

What applies to time applies equally to space. There is no escape from the inexorable measurement of physical space, while the mind can leap about at will so that space and size are arbitrarily determined by thought and feeling. It is only difficult to put a quart into a pint pot in physical space: the mind can do so quite easily.[1]

When we come to dreams, the fluidity of space and time is even more dramatic. In sleep, we seem to be quite detached from absolute measures, and it is well known that a very brief dream, if measured by clock time, can be packed with dramatic incident which might take days or even years of physical life.

This, however, is not the end of the story. For further

---

[1] We do not propose to go into the metaphysical implications of Relativity in this connection. For practical purposes, Euclidian space, and our habit of taking space and time as separate components of the material world is enough.

consideration shows us that the freedom given by the plasticity of mental space-time is indeed only relative. There are occasions on which, unexpectedly, something happens to us which is *really* an experience out of time and space. We will not pause and argue whether it is indeed a vision of a realm where space and time no longer exist at all in an absolute sense: this is unlikely, since something of the nature of space and time must run throughout the gamut of the manifested universe, otherwise there would be no universe. But *to us* it is a valid moment of realisation of a transcendental nature, in which past and future seem to be gathered together in an all-embracing NOW, and all space seems to be present HERE. One can, if one wishes, reverse the description and, instead of suggesting non-extension, consider it as an experience of indefinite extension: both are valid ways of describing the same thing.[1]

Such moments have been described—as far as they can be described—by poets and mystics in all times, and are the experience of people to-day no less than in the past. In fact, they are perhaps commoner to-day, as more and more people become capable of appreciating them. One of their characteristics is unexpectedness. They may come in moments of great exaltation through the perception of beauty, through love or religious devotion, or they may occur in the blackest times of grief or despair. They may be caused by the impact of great events or by some trivial incident in which our perception is changed. In any case, their effect on us is that they bring about some permanent and beneficial change which can only be described as an enlargement of ourselves and of our understanding.

[1]See Warner Allen, *The Timeless Moment.*

What is Man?

'My life was rich, I took a swarm of bees
And found a crumpled snakeskin on the road,
All in one day, and was increased by these.

I have not understood humanity.
But those plain things, that gospel of each year,
Made me the scholar of simplicity.'[1]

Simplicity, union, liberation, bliss, Nirvana, exaltation
coupled with intense humility, the sense of fusion of the
many into the one: all these things are emphasised by
those who have tried, however inadequately, to describe
their experience of this level of their being. But the trouble
in doing so adequately rests in that man's mind is, as yet,
dual and largely unable to place contradictions side by
side and see the wholeness of what, together, they represent. Further, any departure or loosening of consciousness
from the physical frame is accompanied by a sense of
expansion, even though this may be due merely to a
slight degree of hypnosis, the expansion being lost on a
return to normal. The result is that minor psychic experience is often confused with spiritual vision, which it is
not—unless the spiritual quality be superimposed on it.
In any case, reason for the difficulty lies in that the ego
is so much identified with the mind. It, so to speak, normally inhabits the mind and, in waking life, the mind is
usually firmly anchored to the body. It is only rarely that
the ego transcends these, and when it does it is naturally
enough at a loss to translate what it has seen during its
moment of transcendence, into the language with which
it is familiar.

Spiritual experience takes place when the ego has temporarily moved from the level of man which is objective,

[1] V. Sackville West, *The Land*.

extended and explicit, into a realm which is still subjective unextended, and implicit—and this is probably as
good a definition of what we call spirit, not experience,
as can be achieved.

The important point to realise is that, in order to be
able to have an experience of anything, we need the
necessary organism through which it can reach us. That
is, in the case of man, a body to perceive the physical,
material world; a spirit about which we know little except
that it exists and is ours—or perhaps, in the light of
mystical experience, which is more intimately ourselves
than anything we ordinarily call 'I'. This is entirely free
from physical limitations. But it is the 'organ' through
which we know certain phases of experience. Between the
two we have the mind or soul, which is the normal habitat
of our sense of identity. This partakes, in some measure,
of both the attributes of the body and its limitations, and
of the spirit which we only know as unlimited, whether
it be so in fact, or not.

Before passing on to a consideration of the implications
in the scheme of man which we have just outlined, there
is another aspect of him which needs emphasis. We are
used to thinking of ourselves as discrete, self-contained
individuals. Our bodies are limited by a skin which tells
us quite clearly where we end and the outside world begins.
We carry this habit of thought to the psychic level, where
we believe that a similar line of demarcation can be
drawn between our own minds and the minds of others.
This, however, is only partly true: the mind is the child
of both spirit and body and, as we have already said,
the latter is a well defined and shaped unit. But
the essential quality of spirit is union and absence of
division.

What is Man?

The soul of man is thus both individual and self-contained and part of a much larger entity which is known variously as the collective, the herd, the universal mind, and by many other names. All of these suggest the same idea, which is that, whether we know it or not, and whether we like it or not, each one of us is inextricably embedded in a group consciousness which affects the habit of our thoughts and feelings far more than we realise. More about this can be learned from books such as McDougall's *Social Psychology*, Trotter's *Instincts of the Herd in Peace and War*, and the many essays concerned with the collective mind which are to be found in the writings of C. G. Jung. It is also contained in the philosophies of Leibnitz and Bergson, with their concepts of Universal Mind, in which the personal mind of each one of us is a subdivision.

For purposes of the present study, Jung is perhaps the most relevant because he tells us how, at times, the collective can enter into and invade the individual mind, filling it with material and data which belong, not to that individual alone, but to the group of which he is a part. He also tells us much about the richly dramatic and vivid symbolism which belongs to the collective, and how this symbolism can become embodied in the form of figures, both human and not human. These represent forces and principles which have deep spiritual significance yet which, as they appear to individuals, emanate from the deeps of their own being. They are not of the same order as apparitions from outside, such as a ghost or the figure of a dead relative may be. These subjective symbols, which he calls archetypal, include such figures as those of kings, priests, doctors, sages, warriors, and even those of parents or children, whether one's own or those of others.

What is Man?

This is a point to note when it comes to analysing the supposed apparitions of great beings, or even of one's own relatives, in the course of psychic investigation.

This is a very brief summary of Jung's views and by no means does them justice. The point in mentioning them at all is to draw attention to the existence of the collective mind as a thing to be reckoned with in our later studies.

But there is one thing more about the collective, which is not at all clear from Jung's writings. In fact, it may be that, because of the amount of pious nonsense which is talked about good and evil by those who are afraid of instinct and try to escape from it by being 'spiritual', he has purposely avoided the subject so as not to give them a handle with which to misuse his views. This thing is that there are, in effect, two means of contact with the collective, one of which is good and healthy, the other, not so. The difference lies in that the first leads to an increased awareness and a strengthening of the hold of the ego on the conscious field, while the other weakens that hold and so is, from the viewpoint of spiritual progress, a step backward in evolution, towards undifferentiated mass consciousness.

Man's development seems to take place in three stages. First, his consciousness is undifferentiated: he is at much the same level as the animal, unaware of himself, and ruled largely by collective—i.e., in his case, tribal, racial, totemistic—impulses which are much akin to the purely instinctive mandates which govern animal behaviour. Gradually, however, his ego germinates and he becomes an individualist, making his own behaviour-patterns, at first within the framework of the tribal conventions and tabus, later breaking out of them when it suits him to do so. In doing this, as we have already said, he loses the direct, if unconscious, perception of the collective-instinctive levels. From an evolutionary standpoint this is a good thing, provided it leads on to the third stage.

Here, with a firmly established ego, he once more widens out his field and begins to include in it many of the things he has been forced .to shut out during the chrysalis state during which his ego consciousness became formed and well founded. During this intermediate stage, mental and intellectual development take place: he becomes a rational, thinking creature, with all the strength as well as the limitations of perception which this phase brings with it. In the third stage, he learns to come out of the self-made prison of intellect and, if he is to progress further, returns to the same wide perceptive field from which he started— that is, into fusion, into the collective. But there is a vast difference between this state and the original one, in that he now works from the firm centre of his sense of self-identity. The return to the collective shows itself in all the many ways in which the social consciousness is manifesting itself to-day, giving one the feeling that it is wrong to batten on one's fellows, but that one has a duty as well as individual rights where society is concerned and that, to be happy, one must find one's right place in, and contribution to, that society.

The difference between the two stages of the collective consciousness is perhaps best understood by means of an analogy. If a train goes into a tunnel there is a time when the field of vision of those travelling in it is narrowed down to the small, illuminated area of the carriage they are in. Gone are the wide views of fields and woods and sky, until eventually the train reaches open country again. Then once more the same things are seen as before. But in terms of the voluntary road there is the difference that the tunnel now lies behind instead of ahead, while the dark period represents a certain distance travelled and hence a shortening of the distance to the ultimate goal. In other words, something has been accomplished, progress has been made, even though it appeared as though one had lost a great deal of what was precious during the dreary time in the tunnel. Among whatever other passengers there may be on the train there is the personal ego, and for most of us it is still in the tunnel. Our vision of things is dim and narrow, we 'are not psychic', all that we perceive is within the narrow limits of the tunnel itself. But the memory of wider vision is dimly with us as a nostalgia: we know we have had it in some distant Golden Age, and perhaps we feel that we can regain it some day, and there are some who are eagerly trying to find it. We can do so, if we choose, by backing out of the tunnel the way we went in. But this is a retrograde step: the tunnel will still have to be crossed, the darkness must still be faced and conquered. We can, on the other hand, go forward through the dark phase and come out on the other, the positive, side. That is, we can either weaken ourselves and diminish our powers of self-direction, or we can go forward and emerge stronger and with our power of control increased. It is a matter of method which we do.

The analogy can be made more precise if we think of each human being as represented by the whole of the train, not merely by one of the passengers in it. The ego would then be one of the travellers, and the area within the compass of his vision would be what we know as the conscious mind. The rest of the train would then be what the psychologist calls the unconscious. Normally the ego would travel roughly in the middle of the train. But he has freedom to move either towards the engine or towards the guard's van at the rear. This involves some effort but it can be achieved by various practices and the net result is either to lengthen the time spent in the tunnel or to shorten it, according to whether he moves backward or forward along the train. He may even go so far as to come out into the part of the train which has not yet entered the tunnel, and so get a semblance of spiritual vision, soon to be lost when the rear part of the train passes into the darkness.

It is thus obvious that what we do and how we do it is not a matter of merely theoretical importance from the viewpoint of spiritual development. We can, by our own actions either retard or advance the moment of our emergence from the twilight into the light of positive vision and understanding. Where the development of psychic powers are concerned, especially is this an important matter, as we shall see in a later chapter.

2

DO WE SURVIVE?

Consideration of the constitution of man naturally raises many problems with regard to him and his capacities, his past and his future. None is perhaps closer to each one of us, none of greater importance in the conduct of our lives here and now, than our personal conviction about life and death. The argument is often put forward, that if we, as individuals, snuff out like a burned-out candle and nothing is left but a little heap of inert matter, there seems little point in doing anything but leading a comfortable life to the end, undisturbed by ethical, moral, or social problems. If, on the other hand, life is felt to be a continuing and enduring process with limitless possibilities, then the whole matter becomes at once more difficult and complex, and vastly more interesting and purposeful. This applies even if one holds the common belief that one only has one life on earth, which is followed by a problematical aftermath of one kind or another.

Can we draw any conclusions about the problem? This is extremely difficult to do objectively, because the answer must, of necessity, be influenced by our personal desires. Some would think it a most comforting notion that their

Do We Survive?

troubles ended at the moment of death. Others cling to the idea of continuing life as *themselves*: they dread the idea of losing their little ego which is the only thing they know that gives them a sense of identity. Again, to others, the idea of continuing is pleasant, provided they make a good job of their earthly life and can therefore hope for eternal rest, whether in the Elysian Fields or in some form of conventional heaven; but they reject with loathing the idea that they may have to reincarnate and go on striving. Many people are, of course, terrified of the very idea of death, and do not stop to consider whether they have another chance or not. Their terror of surrendering their sense of self is such that anything is preferable to total extinction. So the whole subject becomes deeply coloured by one's personal emotional reactions, many of which are barely conscious and may even be deeply unconscious. But these factors condition the conscious attitude to the problem.

There are comparatively few people who are able to analyse the alternatives objectively and reach, as a result, some deep inner conviction in the matter—which is the only means of finding any certainty or security about it. For, and this should be written in capital letters, there is no scientific proof of survival, no matter what spiritualists and psychical researchers may say. It is true that there is a great deal of evidential material, enough, in fact, to justify the belief. But it is circumstantial evidence and hence suggestive rather than definite, and it does not constitute scientific proof. This evidence tilts the scales heavily in favour of survival, but at the purely intellectual level, it must be admitted that there is room for considerable doubt.

Equally, there is no scientific proof that the death of a man's body is the end of that man, no matter what materialists may assert. Moreover, the further one pursues the study of man and the powers of his mind, the more unlikely it becomes that any such *proof* will be found, while individual *conviction* in this direction is likely to increase. Likewise, the more we understand of psychology the more we discover that popular belief is often founded on an intuition of truth, even though that truth may suffer something of a change in the process of being expounded as general doctrine. This applies to the age-old belief in survival.

In the course of the last century, a number of scientists of repute have tried to devise tests of survival which would put the matter beyond doubt either way. Manuscripts, for instance, have been written, sealed into packets and deposited with a bank unread by any but their writer. The idea was that, if the writer survived the death of his body, he would try, through mediums or any available channel, to reproduce what he had written in his earthly life. The packets would eventually be withdrawn from the safe and opened, in the hope that the material communicated would be at least near enough to the original to be convincing. But let us assume that a medium, or an automatic writer, reproduced exactly and word for word the manuscript which had lain for twenty years in obscurity. This proves only one thing, which is that the medium is being a channel for material psychically perceived. For, while it might indeed be dictated or directly communicated by the original writer from the posthumous world, we also know, from laboratory experiments in clairvoyance, that it is quite possible for a sensitive person to read letters in a closed envelope, and that walls and doors are no obstacle. Hence the medium might very well have read the manuscript directly. Or, alternatively, he might quite possibly have precognised the words which would at a later time be read by him, or by the person who would open the packet in the safe. All this may sound far-fetched to readers who are not accustomed to the subject, but, as investigators of long standing will know, these things are not only possible but have actually been accomplished.

Hence proof under test conditions tends to fall to the ground because there are so many other possible explanations. The same applies to communications such as are common to all spiritualistic circles—the nature of which is analysed in a later chapter.

On the other hand we have, as already pointed out, the belief, which is practically universal, that survival is the natural order of things. This is borne out by innumerable stories of apparitions, hauntings, and personal experiences, *all* of which are not likely to be untrue. We need to remember, too, that whatever our wishes in the matter may be, it does not follow that *because* we wish for a thing it is *therefore* ruled out. There is, moreover, something to be deduced from the analysis of man made in the first chapter. This analysis is philosophical but, if the premises about the structure of the human being are correct, the rest must follow. These arguments undoubtedly show a personal bias, but they may reasonably be put forward as a basis from which to work.

Man, as we have suggested, lives in his body in a world ruled by absolute time. Time passes and the body, geared into the time-track, is born, grows, deteriorates, and dies. His mind or soul lives in contact with that time-track and hence must be relatively mortal. But it is also anchored to the spiritual principle, which seems to be outside time. It is inconceivable that anything outside of time can be mortal. It would be a contradiction logically quite untenable that anything which is not subject to the inevitable movement and change which is the law of time, should yet be dragged along through the cyclic phases of birth and mortality which time forces on her subjects. On the other hand the mystical experience is entirely convincing that spirit lives in eternity, which is saying the same thing the other way about. Hence the soul, being the child of immortal spirit as well as of mortal flesh, must also be relatively enduring. That is, it survives the death of the time-bound body, but it does not partake of the eternal existence of the spirit.

What would this mean in practice? That the soul of man, after the death of the body, may very well retain for a time many of its earthly characteristics, but that it does not do so for ever. Thus a dead person communicating with a living one, soon after his death, will appear very much what he was in life. True, he will have shed the limitations of consciousness which the physical frame imposes, and he will probably be more aware in the region of what was his unconscious mind. But this by no means sets him free altogether, or gives him much more wisdom than he had before. He remains essentially human as we understand the term, and does not become an illumined teacher or saint.

The question then arises as to whether he remains where he is. Once more the principles put forward suggest that he does not, because his soul belongs at once to the timeless and to the world of time. And since he has, so to speak, let go of time, it is reasonable to suppose that there is likely to be a definite pull towards the timeless spiritual principle between which and the time-body his ego was held in balance during life. Hence this ego will tend to pass on towards the spiritual or timeless state. To do so must involve a gradual liquidation of those attributes of himself which belong to time and the material world. That is, those which belong to the earth-surface of himself, and which we describe as his personality.

It is, of course, impossible to postulate any period of earth-time for this process. But, in so far as the person's nature was earthy, it is reasonable to imagine that the period in terms of earth-time will be longer than that of a person whose interests and aspirations were less material and more idealistic and abstract. Eventually—bearing in mind the relative mortality of the soul—one may postulate that the ego-consciousness removes itself altogether from the soul-level: that the soul in turn dies and the cycle of life resolves itself in a return to the timelessness of pure spirit. We thus have something akin to the Christian doctrine of a purgatorial state. It is also in line with the more explicit teachings of Ancient Egypt, Tibet, Buddhism, and Hinduism.

It suggests, moreover, that that which is permanent and eternal in man is not his personality, not that collection of habits and attitudes of mind and blind spots of understanding, but his spirit, and that only.

It may very well be objected that if spirit, an abstraction, as it were, is all that survives, then what use or value is there in personal life, with all the stress and suffering it entails? But man's soul is an aggregate of the qualities of both the material and the spiritual nature, and, as such, some of the qualities of the personality must belong to the spiritual nature. Hence we may assume that those spiritual attributes remain with him and become integrated with the permanent part of himself; that is to say, whatever is real about his religion, his artistry, his love for others, his courage and all those things which we respect as much as we may deprecate the negative

44

qualities. (It should be noted that it is what is *real* about these things, not the spurious and the merely goody-goody, which can be considered spiritual. There is a great deal of apparent altruism and virtue which in reality springs from self-interest of one kind or another, not from truly disinterested motives.)

Hence it may be that *personal* immortality is indeed a myth. But *individual* immortality is one of the deepest truths of life. For the personality, made up of mental and physical characteristics of a person, belongs to the changing world of time, whereas the individuality consists of those enduring qualities which belong to the spirit of man and of which, as the word itself tells us, the personality or mask-self is only the outer garment.

One point, however, emerges from this. If man has, indeed, a part of him which lives in the eternal, we cannot logically think of it as existing now and in the future, but not in the past. Therefore, one must assume that the new-born child, considered as spirit, must have existed in the past as he will in days to come. What of that past? And, for the matter of that, what of the future?

We come here to the point where the logical development of our argument must be more speculative. We know very little about time, and we know that in a certain sense time is an illusion. Thus it may well be that all the past and future existence of life in the time-world is taking place at once, but that our temporal mind sorts that experience out and lays it along the time-track as a convenient way of looking at it, with the present as a dot running along the track, away from what we call the past towards what we call the future. For practical purposes, however, this possible fiction will have to suffice.

Further, from the time-track level of consciousness, the

physical, it seems that life ever moves in cycles or, in scientific language, it is phasic. If that is so, then it is not unreasonable to suppose that the stages from birth, through the noonday of physical life, to death and onwards are balanced against another phase from the midnight of death outwards towards the time of birth, thus completing the cycle. If this is so, we should then see the spiritual man, seemingly out of time, projecting himself repeatedly into time, then withdrawing again until he reaches some climacteric of experience of time, and is free. Whether this would take place on earth, as believed by reincarnationists, or whether the cycles of experience take place elsewhere is a more doubtful matter. But, in any case, it would make sense if it were on earth or some place like it.

All this argument may be a kind of logical scaffolding to push away a latent fear of extinction. On the other hand, it may also represent a bridge between materialism and those who insist on some form of immortality, in that it does away with personal survival, yet allows of the immortality of the spirit which is man.

To some extent it may also be held to suggest that when man dies, his personal mind and experience return to the pool of the collective and only survive in so far as they affect that collective. For he is a part of the collective when he is dead just as much as when he is alive: the life of individual man is always a part of the life of collective Man, wherever he may be in his experience. This is a doctrine at least implicit in the conception of universal mind put forward by such philosophers as Leibnitz and Bergson. But, more than that, those who have had a vision of spiritual life know this as a fact, not merely as a hypothesis, because one attribute of this vision is the unity of every living creature. At that level there is One and not many, and all things are shared.

Before closing this chapter, it may be as well to mention the matter of those who purport to remember their past lives, or who—usually uninvited—tell other people of theirs.

Naturally, where one's own memories are concerned, personal conviction has the last word. But there are a number of points which need to be considered. First of all there is imagination and one's power to evoke images in the mind, either about oneself or about others. It is very easy, for instance, to describe somebody as a typical cavalier, or an old witch from mediaeval times, simply because they look the part and have some of its characteristics to-day. It is only going one step further to embroider the theme and to weave it into a story, and thence to believe that that story is true and is the memory of someone else's past life. Similarly, it is comforting to oneself to think that one has been a colourful and important person in the past, especially if one is now leading a dull office life in a city, under grey skies. The compensatory nature of most such 'memories' is too blatant to need emphasis. On the other hand, the fact remains that those memories might be genuine, even though they be pleasant. Again there is no proof; only personal conviction can assess them.

An unusual example of such remembering was given by a friend of ours who was taken seriously ill while staying in the older part of Florence. While he was half delirious, with a high temperature, he lived in a most vivid and personal way through scenes which seemed to be those of his own life in mediaeval Italy. If the nurse came into the room, he was able to pay attention to the present and to answer questions. But the moment he was alone again he slipped into the other life, and picked up his threads, going straight on from where he had left off. In this story, he was a quite well-known person in those times, and had had a highly dramatic life. In the re-living, however, there was an intensity and a richness of detail which, though the main outline of the life of the person was known, he must have supplied himself. Thus on one occasion he overheard a remark in French, between two people in the daydream, whereas previous talk had been in Italian. This showed him that an emotional relationship to a certain woman, who had been one of the main characters in the dream, was still alive long after he had thought it was finished. This was to him, in his mediaeval character, a considerable shock. Likewise he described his handling of parchment documents, feeling the texture of them, the roughness of the wax seals, and many other small details. When the illness cleared up, he came out of the spell, though the vivid memories remained.

The uncritical reincarnationist would most likely say at once that he was remembering a past life. But careful examination leaves even so dramatic an incident in doubt. To begin with, the setting was appropriate to the scenes played out. The man himself was a deep student of mediaeval history, and had always been attracted to the writings of the particular person with whom he identified himself during the illness. Further, the man was in that peculiar state of high fever when all impressions acquire an enhanced vividness. So that, altogether, the stage was set for such a dramatisation to take place.

In this it differs from memories which are only too common in which people claim to have been Pharaohs or great people: there was no self-exaltation in this vision, so that the question has to be left open. In any case, the past is really unimportant in comparison with the present and how we are steering the ship of our lives to-day. Hence it is usually great waste of time and energy to dwell too much on unproven memories out of a mythical past. On the other hand, there are times when a sequential drama, expressed in terms of a series of lives, may have a real value to the person concerned and help him to solve a present-day psychological problem. In such a case, whether they be historically true or whether they represent a kind of allegorical drama imagined by the individual, is of minor importance. What does matter is that the individual learns from them something which helps him to a greater degree of integration to-day and for the future.[1]

Thus the conclusion seems justifiable that man is in essence immortal and eternal. He is spirit, and this spirit, for purposes beyond our understanding, projects some part of itself into the extended worlds of matter, space and time. It seems unlikely and unreasonable, however, to think that the span between the birth and death of one body can represent the whole of the space-time experience of spiritual man: the extraordinary maturity of some children even at a very early age, and the high degree of psychological development of the most ordinary person, itself points to this being improbable. On the other hand, these things suggest that such experience may have begun before physical birth and may extend beyond the death of the body.

Further, Nature appears to work according to a cyclic or phasic law. Wherever one looks, vibration—that is,

[1] See H. K. Challoner, *The Wheel of Rebirth*: a novel based on the theme of a chain of incarnations.

Do We Survive?

movement between opposite and complementary poles—
is the rule. The whole material world depends for its
existence upon such movement: we see it whether we look
at the celestial bodies or at the chemical atom, and at
every stage between these two. There is no reason to
suppose that man is any exception, and it would follow
from this that his material experience is likely to alternate
between phases of activity and latency in the world where
the phasic law holds good. This would mean periodic
change from outward-turned action to inward-turned
withdrawal, just as he does during life when he sleeps and
wakes from one day to the next. In terms of a greater cycle,
this would mean an alternation between incarnation and
non-incarnation, taking place not once only, but repeatedly.

This theory is one which, apart from being very widely
held, makes sense, and would explain the many apparent
anomalies between people of different capacity and temperament; and, if it is true, it does away with any idea of
injustice on the part of the Creator, whatever name we give
to him: Nature, Natural Law, or God. On the contrary, it
brings man under the sway of natural law and of the balancing up of forces and energies, at all levels of creation. Hence,
it seems a comfortable theory from the intellectual point of
view, as well as one giving a practical philosophy of life.

And this, perhaps, is the very thing which should make
us suspicious of it, for it may be merely a subtle form of
wishful thinking. It may be that materialism is right,
that the universe is a fortuitous thing, that man is simply
a body, though a most elaborate one. But somehow this
does not, for many people, seem to fit the facts of their own
experience any more than do those of a vague orthodox
religion. There is no certainty about such things except
that which the individual develops from within himself.

3

NEGATIVE AND POSITIVE PSYCHISM

In previous chapters it has been suggested that the evolutionary process in man leads him from undifferentiated consciousness towards differentiation and the establishment of a firm centre of that consciousness in the ego. This ego-centre gives him clarity of focus in the conscious field, and a high degree of control over it. He increases the control of himself by enlarging the field which comes under the aegis of the ego—that is, by including, step by step, more of his unconscious mind.

One may go a step further by suggesting that until the ego becomes established, in however a rudimentary a manner, there is nothing there except the unconscious. That is, the conscious mind only begins to exist when the possibility of knowing the difference between 'I' and 'Not-I' becomes manifest. At first the conscious field is narrow; the little ego has to begin at the beginning and can only handle a small amount of material at a time. Hence in primitive man the personal life is very much restricted, the tribal or collective life being the dominant factor and running very much along instinctive lines. Gradually, however, the field of the ego enlarges, and the line of demarcation between it and the unconscious becomes

51

more definite. But to achieve this means the deletion from the conscious field of a great deal of mental equipment—such as direct response to instinctive guidance. Only in this way do we achieve clarity of focus and purpose within the field. As Bergson points out, we limit ourselves in order to overcome evolutionary difficulties, just as water going through the narrow nozzle of a hose acquires power, or as a nation at war cuts down much that is of general value to put all its energies into the main purpose, survival.

Thus man, in the middle phase of his evolution, reaches a climacteric point of maximum limitation in every direction, and also of maximum power within that limited field. This is probably the state of individualism, of power politics, of purely materialistic scientific and technical achievement—a phase in which we are still largely plunged. Beyond this stage lies the next one, when once again man can begin to expand, when he is so rational and objective that he can safely step beyond rationalism and objectivity, and begin—as psychology is doing to-day—to bring into his ken that which was hitherto irrational and unobjective, and hence dangerous to his mental evolution. Science can now afford to take into its orbit subjective material and speculations which are not within the reach of material proof.

Thus progress lies first in deletion of parts of the mind, then in bringing back into consciousness that which was deleted. But the bringing back must lead, not to a weakening of the egoic control but, on the contrary, to a widening of the field over which that control is exercised. The result is that man becomes increasingly self-directed and able to choose for himself what he will do and how.

The ethical questions involved in all this are not our concern in this chapter, which has to do with the perceptive aspects of man. For among other things which

Negative and Positive Psychism

are deleted during the establishment of self-consciousness is a great deal of his ability to perceive what is going on around him. At first sight this may seem to be a pity, but from an evolutionary standpoint it is a good thing. For the physical world is solid and fixed in a way in which the psychic is not, while the spiritual is known only as non-spatial, non-temporal and, being unextended, is incapable of giving spirit-man whatever advantages accrue from his incarnation in extended space-time.

The clarity of the physical world enables man to anchor and focus his mentality in a way the psychic cannot because of its plasticity. His perceptive function has, in the physical world, something to bite on, something which offers resistance to his mind, while the psychic world so readily adapts itself to thought and feeling that it offers no fulcrum. Hence man, obscuring the psychic aspects of his perceptivity, finds in the physical world somewhere in which to perfect that part of the perceptive faculty which belongs to it. This in its turn, by giving him a clear and definite line of demarcation between 'I' and 'Not-I', strengthens and consolidates his ego, and leads to the power of objective thinking most characteristically seen in the scientific and logical mind of to-day.

But beyond the turning point, and once such objectivity has become a permanent power of the mind, he once more needs to bring into the field in which controlled and objective thinking is possible, all the things which he has temporarily pushed aside. This includes that aspect of perception which we call psychism or the Psi function.

These principles give us a direct clue to the radical difference between negative and positive psychism. It also shows us the difference between positive and negative forms of development of psychic perceptivity. These are

53

not the same thing, because the two orders of psychism are respectively like the bottom and top of a hill, whereas a person half-way up the hill can reach the bottom either by the method of letting himself go and rolling or sliding down out of control, or he may make an orderly and deliberate descent. To reach the top, however, he needs effort and hard work, and nothing will waft him up by accident.

Negative psychism is the psychism of the primitive. It is part of a general faculty of perceptivity which embraces both the physical and the psychic realms, and, moreover, it covers both the subjective contents of the mind and things outside it. At this level perceptivity is an inchoate and undifferentiated function without barriers or demarcation between parts and regions.

To the savage such general perceptivity is normal and natural. Perception flows into his mind unchecked and unsorted, and this is probably one reason for his extraordinary and subtle response to what is going on around him, both at the physical and psychic levels. He is not preoccupied with himself—having little self with which to be preoccupied—and hence he does not shut himself up within himself. But the civilised man of to-day has created a more or less closed field around his ego, thereby shutting out much of what might otherwise be awareness of the surrounding world about him. He naturally focuses on the material world, and whatever he perceives, belongs to that level. In large measure, too, he knows how to control and direct his perceptivity in this field to his own ends. He listens to what he wants to hear, looks at a particular object and at little else, he selects from his environment what he requires to observe at any particular moment. Yet, as we have already said, the whole of the perceptive function remains in civilised man, even though for evolutionary purposes a barrier tends to arise between the hard physical and the fluidic psychic worlds.

All this is part of the development of man's ego as a focus of conscious and deliberate control of his life in the space-time world. Hence positive psychism, when once more he begins to widen his perceptive field must of necessity have precisely those qualities of conscious control, of clear focus and selectivity which now belong, at least in some measure to the physical senses alone.

Most of mankind, at any rate in the West, are on the slopes of the hill. With the possible exception of the few Australian aborigines and such people, few human beings are altogether at the bottom of the hill, and if any have reached the summit, they must be classed among the gods, and are no longer ordinary men. So any one of us has the option of travelling upward or downward, and where the perceptive function is concerned there is a decided difference between the methods which lead in one direction or the other.

A word may usefully be said at this point about those people who either consider themselves, or are considered by others, to be exceptional because of their psychic perceptivity, whether this acts in full consciousness or in the less desirable condition of mediumistic trance. They are not in any way unusual in having received special gifts from Providence. Psychic perceptivity is an endowment of every human being, whether it be latent or active. The 'psychic' is only different in that he has a special facility for making a conscious link with the psychic world—just as others have a special facility for languages or mathematics—and nothing more.

In general, anything which tends to diminish the conscious control of the ego is negative or regressive, while anything which helps it to widen the field under its control is positive or teleological. Where psychic perceptivity is concerned, anything which tends to re-open the psychic field otherwise than under direct control, is negative, whereas conscious and deliberate addition to the area which is now largely limited to the physical world, is positive.

We may continue to use the analogy of the hillside to suggest that the disorderly fall down the slope is where illness, drugs, alcohol, shocks, or over-fatigue, as well as the results of unconscious hypnotism—e.g. from repetitive sounds like the noise of a train over the rails, or native drums—opens up some form of involuntary psychic perception. But, as perceptivity this is usually inextricably mixed up with the subjective mental contents of the mind, the result is often a kind of phantasmagoria, sometimes interesting and pleasant, sometimes nightmarish. These visions and experiences can be nothing but confusion, or on the other hand they can be clear and sequential, as in the case of the sick man in Florence; but whatever the results the experience is undirected and erratic.

The deliberate descent, however, is that which results from either 'sitting for development' or the practice of Hatha Yoga exercises designed for the purpose of stimulating the psychic function. The effect of these is to carry man back along the evolutionary path, at least temporarily, and to place him at a level of consciousness lower than that at which he normally functions. This needs explanation, because it will be argued that a person in a half-way state or 'under control' is in touch with a greater and wider consciousness. It is lower in that the control of the ego is lessened, and this despite the fact that in this condition a higher and more enlightened level of the medium's personality may become manifest. The conscious mind of the medium is so much concentrated on ordinary things that

Negative and Positive Psychism

it is only in this loosened condition that higher functions can make themselves felt. The psychologist, therefore, as he is concerned with the mental health of people, must of necessity look upon negative methods as unwise, to say the least of it, no matter how interesting the results may be. Such methods include those of trance medium-ship, Hatha Yoga exercises, the use of drugs or hypnosis, whether self-induced or induced by another operator.

Positive methods, however, are aimed at precisely the same thing as sound psychological training, or the Raja Yoga of India and the equivalent in all other religions; that is, at increased conscious perception with increased self-direction, aiming at a spiritual goal.

This high-sounding definition may seem very remote from immediate and practical purposes. But what it amounts to is this: that the person who wants to develop his psychic perceptivity on healthy lines needs to be interested in knowledge and understanding of life and the principles which underlie it. He needs to feel there is some plan or purpose in existence which is more important than just his own personal development and self-interest. Thus he is not satisfied with merely using his perceptivity for such things as giving messages, descriptions of dead people and their supposed activities, or even in transmitting ethical communications. He wants to learn the truth about things, and experience them directly for himself. Second-hand experience is no longer of any use to him, he has an urge to forge ahead and find his own.

This means hard work and self-discipline, and, most painful of all, the growth of self-knowledge which only arrives after gradual elimination of many cherished illusions. He works at clearing the field of his ego from its egoism, even at the risk, it would seem, of losing the ego itself.

Negative and Positive Psychism

Thus we arrive at the important question 'What do I want to do?' and 'What am I after?', and it is an important matter that people who are urged, either by their own wishes or the persuasions of other people, to 'sit for development' should seriously ask themselves what is their goal. Too many people want to 'become psychic' at any price. Their motives differ. It may be that they want to use their gifts to make money, or to gain power. Some feel that it is rather distinguished, or that they can be of great service to others. Some feel a vague notion, or have a strong feeling that, if they are psychic, they also gain spiritual insight—which is quite another matter. Others are idealistic, and feel that they will be helping the world and bringing comfort to many. But none of these reasons is quite good enough, nor is it likely to give real satisfaction, because the only way to see things straight and correctly, whether in the physical or psychic worlds, comes after long self-training, much hard work, and many disappointments. Few people are serious enough to be willing to undertake that work: they want quick results and something more spectacular and exciting than the quiet, slow development of their spiritual qualities. For the truly spiritual person—the only one who can be relied upon—is not necessarily psychic at all, in the sense of being explicitly clairvoyant or clairaudient. He will certainly be too wise to develop negative mediumistic practices, knowing that there are better ways of helping both himself and other people. Nor will he make claims about his powers, or feel himself to be superior to others, because spiritual pride is the negation of spiritual quality.

On the other hand, as a person grows in spiritual insight, as a result of intensive self-training, his perceptive field naturally widens and enlarges. He finds himself becoming psychic in the true sense, but his interest is in the spiritual value more than the psychic vision, useful though the psychic aspect may be to him. Positive psychism must, therefore, in the nature of things, appear only as secondary, a side-issue, so to speak, to a deeper quest for truth. It is true that it may, for some, be one of the main instruments in their search. But unless their prime motive is truth, *not* the development of psychism as such, they are bound to frustrate themselves before long.

It is possible to go a long way in the field of the physical sciences without bothering about the spiritual aspects of life, for here one has objective standards against which to correct and gauge one's work. But even here, eventually, these are not enough and the deeper side has to be brought in. In the sphere of psychic science, however—whether in the subjective field of the psychologist or in that of the objectively perceptive psychic—there are no such standards, and the inevitable result of the lack of a spiritual touchstone is unreliability, inaccuracy, confusion, and, more often than not, self-inflation. Hence, the person who is ambitious to be a good psychic needs to take stock of himself before trying to embark on any scheme of development. It is well if he looks first and foremost at his true purpose. And, if it is psychism which interests him rather than Life itself, he will do well to leave it alone, and to confine himself to learning to know himself as he is, not to try prematurely to develop capacities which are so easily deceptive.

Nearly all methods used in mediumistic circles tend towards a less clear-cut control of the personality—a form of self-abdication rather than self-control, whereas wise and positive training leads naturally to a greater integration of the personal life, as well as to greater and truer vision.

4

GHOSTS AND HAUNTS

The idea that certain places are haunted is as old as mankind. Materialistic science naturally tended to dismiss the idea as one of the superstitions which impeded human progress, but, in view of the careful investigation of individual cases, it has had to change its tone somewhat. There seems little doubt that strange things do occur at times, and these are constant enough to give story-writers a foothold on reality when they try to curdle the blood of their readers. There are many different types of apparitions and of haunts, and the question arises as to whether they are all due to the same causes, or whether they represent different phenomena with only one common factor—that they are an intrusion from the psychic realm into that of ordinary material objects and events. If, for instance, an old house is haunted by the figure of a monk wandering down the passages, is the monk himself there? Or is it only some remnant of him? Or is the observer merely tapping the 'memory' of the house itself? And is this the same thing as where a certain vivid scene appears to be re-enacted on a certain day of the year, to be perceived by those sleeping in a particular room? Again, how do these things differ from the phenomena occurring in some houses where, no matter how carefully a door may be locked, and even closed with screws, it is always open on the following morning? And yet again, is there any radical difference between the harmless haunt and the one which seems potentially harmful and malicious? And is a single, sudden apparition the same thing as a repeated and long-standing haunt?

Several good and many indifferent books have been written on the subject of apparitions.[1] The evidence that such things are genuine, and the careful analysis of the way they take place and how they appear to people—sometimes seemingly transparent, sometimes opaque and so on—is admirable, but the problem as to their nature and the mechanism which produces them remains.

To this there is no simple answer, but the experience of psychics suggests that in each case there are a number of possibilities. Even though what follows must of necessity be speculative, it is worth pursuing as a matter of general interest. The subject falls under two main headings. One is the apparition of somebody a long way away. If the person be alive and not within obvious reach of death, then he is likely to be unconscious either as a result of sleep, drugs, anaesthesia or accident. The person who appears in such a manner is usually at some critical period of life: near death, or undergoing some serious ordeal, but this is not necessarily so. Indeed there are many instances on record where a person in perfectly good health and undergoing no particular stress, has been seen by somebody else, usually a friend a long way off, yet it seemed as if the apparition were in the same room as the observer.

[1] See, for instance, among the good ones: G. N. M. Tyrrell, *Apparitions*, published by the Society for Psychical Research; Gurney, Myers, Podmore, *Phantasms of the Living*.

Ghosts and Haunts

Here is an account of an instance which demonstrates this, and which has the additional and unusual feature that both parties, the one who 'went' and the one who saw the psychic apparition, were aware of the event, and corroborated one another at a later date.

'Many years ago I had an unusual experience. For some time I had been pondering over a problem of psychic technique, and wondered which of my friends had enough skilled knowledge to help me. Suddenly I remembered a man who was on the far side of Europe. He was a soldier, psychically sensitive, and possessed more knowledge than I had myself.

'As I thought of him, it was almost as though I had closed an electric switch. Though I sat in my own room in England, alert, and in full waking consciousness, it seemed as though a part of my mind travelled out through space. In a few seconds I felt as though I were in two places at once. The stationary "me" was aware of the room I was in, the rough texture of the chair-cover under my fingers, and all the usual things surrounding me; but the travelling part of my mind seemed to shoot through space, rather like an arrow winging its way to a target. In what seemed like a flash of time this moving part of me found itself in a place it had never seen. It was a bare office. I carefully noted the position of the door, the window, filing cabinets, and large office table. Seated at a desk, writing, was my friend, dressed in uniform.

'The strange thing that struck me at the time was that, although he continued to write, some part of his mind appeared to know that I was there, and at once a telepathic rapport was set up which, in some odd fashion, enabled me mentally to discuss my problem with him. His mind grasped what was needed, and quickly gave me

62

the answer I wanted. As soon as this happened the telepathic line of communication was switched off, and I had
a queer feeling of my mind returning along the track by
which it had gone out.

'Not knowing what to make of this vivid experience, I
immediately drew a plan of the office in which I had been,
marking the correct places of the furniture, door and
windows. This I posted to a woman who lived in the same
city as my military friend. She knew us both, so I wrote
explaining what had happened, but I did not tell her the
nature of the problem which had been unravelled.

'About six months later she came to England, and when
we met she said, "Your plan of Jan's room was absolutely
correct. He told me to tell you that he had not only been
mentally aware of your presence, but was quite clear about
the difficulty you were in." She then told me the problem
itself, so that we were able to check the correctness of
what Jan had reported.

'There had always existed a strong mental affinity
between myself and this particular friend, but it was the
only time it operated in this way and at a long distance.'

Of two possibilities in such cases, one is that because of
some strong emotional situation an existing telepathic
rapport is activated between the parties so that one of
them virtually sees the other at a distance. The analogy
with television suggests itself, the image being projected
along the channel already made as a result of affection
and mental rapport between those concerned.

The other possibility links with what has been already
put forward about the objective existence of the psyche
even when detached from the body. If that is so, then
the idea of what some people call 'astral travelling' must
be allowed for: that is, the notion that a person detached

from the body can travel through what we know physically as space, and visit other places than that where his body is. The scientific evidence for such a thing is sketchy, to say the least of it. There are, however, some cases on record which, despite flaws, point to such an explanation. In addition, there is a relatively common experience of people under anaesthetics or physically unconscious who realise that they are actually conscious and able to think and feel at another level, and even see their inert body on the bed or in the dentist's chair. Sometimes they realise themselves as floating in the air, watching the scene below them as if they were detached spectators. Then, perhaps gradually or perhaps in an instant, they find themselves back in their bodies. In one instance, a girl saw her body on the bed and noted changes in the furniture in her room. Then, in her own words, she 'lost consciousness' save for a rather feeble awareness of her surroundings through a body seriously ill with pneumonia. The sense of limitation imposed by entering the flesh is not uncommon in such cases. That means they seem to exist as individuals even apart from their physical bodies.

It does not follow by any means, therefore, that if one should suddenly see an apparition, whether of somebody one knows and loves—or hates—or of a stranger, that that person is dead. Nor does it necessarily mean that he is present in the region of space which is covered by the range of the eyes. The apparition may, in fact, be an image projected from afar. This is usually a fortuitous occurrence, but in principle a really expert person, such as a developed yogi can do these things at will. (It should be added that such things are *not* learned from the organisations which advertise lessons in 'astral projection', at so many dollars a course.)

Ghosts and Haunts

Ghosts and hauntings are something different from the above because they are usually associated with a particular place, or with a particular period of time, such as the full moon or the day of the year, which is the anniversary of a certain event. They may also be aroused by a certain set of circumstances. As we very well know, most people are frightened or curious about them, and, moreover, it is usually taken for granted that the thing which haunts is the soul of a dead human being.

Beyond evidence that there are such things as haunts, psychical research has, however, not yet done much to explain matters. People with personal psychic experience, however, have more suggestive material to contribute to the question, even though it is not susceptible to proof.

For one thing, they know that very many more places are haunted than people imagine. Almost every old house or building, and indeed a good many relatively modern ones have something in them which one might call a ghost. This is not realised, first because relatively few haunts are sufficiently powerful to make ordinary people conscious of them, and secondly, because so many of them are innocuous. It is only when they are at once unpleasant and strong that people become aware of them, and this adds a great deal to the fear which people have of a thing they feel to be uncanny and unnatural.

> 'As I was going up the stair
> I met a man who wasn't there.
> He wasn't there again to-day.
> I wish to God he'ld go away.'

A first principle concerning haunts is that they all seem to be the result of human agency, but that the ghost is not necessarily a human being at all. That is to say, although a human being has created or has left behind at death something of himself, it does not follow that the man himself is there in the form of the ghost: he may be, or he may not.

The second principle is that what becomes the ghost is that part of a man's mind which is attached to the particular place that it haunts. This may be a memory, that is, the thoughts connected with a particular event or series of events, or it may be the whole of the mind of the man concerned. For, as we know, the mind can split itself up into separate sections, so that it is possible for one or more of these sections to be related to the place haunted while the rest of the mind goes free. It is as if the mind were able to shed its contents and leave them behind when itself has passed on elsewhere.

Thus, if some highly dramatic scene takes place in a house—a murder, a death, a lovers' parting—then it seems as if what remains is a strong picture of that event. We may take it either that the event has impressed itself on the place leaving a psychic impression in the room; or that the mind of the participants has shed a part of itself there, just as one might leave a cloak or a ring where one has been. This principle is not without support from physiological investigations which tell us that the physical brain emits electrical waves and radiations. These radiations represent energy and differ only in detail from those we know, let us say as heat. If heat leaves traces, there seems no reason why mental processes should not also leave characteristic marks in a place.

These haunts would represent something emanating from the mind while that mind had itself passed on. Whately Carington's views are apt in this connection.[1]

[1] See his book, *Telepathy.*

Ghosts and Haunts

He postulates that the mind consists of a number of units or *psychons* held together into an integrated whole. The psychon is very much the same as a psychological complex, though viewed differently. One may imagine that when a person has, through whatever circumstances, become strongly associated with a place, the psychon which relates to that place becomes to some extent anchored there. If then a time comes when the psychon becomes detached from the parent-mind, it will tend to stay in the place to which it is already attached. Moreover, it will carry in it a certain charge of energy. It is as if one took apart the several cells of an electric battery: each cell would have its own quota of electric energy which would keep it 'live' until exhausted. The analogy is crude and very material, but it can serve as a symbol of something which fits the facts.

The case we are about to relate is of interest because the 'ghost' was that of a man alive and well, and, at the hour when he was seen, probably engaged in business in his office. It was as follows:

'One summer a friend was lent a bungalow on the cliffs of a small place in Cornwall and invited us to share it. It consisted of a large converted army hut, and had a pleasant sitting-room looking out to sea. There was no particular atmosphere attached to the place, but it was free and easy, and essentially a holiday house. We ourselves had never met the owner.

'One day, while passing the open door of the sitting-room, I casually glanced in. On the hearthrug, with his back to the fireplace, stood a conventionally dressed man of middle age. His hair was carefully parted, his clothes those of a professional man, and he was absorbed in reading a book. I went on along the passage, finished the small

Ghosts and Haunts

job I had on hand, and returned to the open sitting-room door. The man still stood quietly reading. I took careful stock of him, and as I did so, he faded out.

'At the time I did not mention the visitor, but a day or two later the party were discussing psychical research—with Whately Carington and his wife, as it happens—and, to illustrate a point, I told the story of the man I had seen. At that, the one to whom the bungalow had been especially lent, exclaimed, "Oh, but that is a perfect description of Mr. —— who owns this place. He is a bank manager and he reads a great deal."

'The problem is an interesting one. Was the owner of the place thinking about it? Did he project a mental picture of himself into the correct environment? Or did my friend, who was cooking in the back of the house, during the time I saw the man, create and project the figure by her own thought? Did I read her mind?'

There appear to be other instances, however, where what seem to be the whole collection of psychons which make up a person's mind stay in one place, the reason being that the whole life of the person centred entirely around it. Most normal people are attached in some measure to their homes, but their minds have other interests too. That is to say, while some psychons are attached to the house they live in, others are not, and 'belong' elsewhere. But certain recluses, melancholics and people who live quite out of touch with the world may withdraw entirely into their little environment, and it is literally true to say that their whole minds are centred there.

During physical life there seems always to be the possibility that a person may detach himself from a place and carry his psychons with him. But after physical death it seems as if such change were more difficult. The psychon or collection of psychons may become divorced from the ego of the personality to which they belong, and tend to gravitate around the object to which they are attached. If it represents only a part of the mind, then there is only something akin to a memory-picture left. But if the whole personality was centred around the house, then it is as if a complete human being were there, following the old routine of his life, unaware even of having lost his dense body. In fact, we have here the thing which is sometimes described as a dead person 'earth-bound'. Here is a characteristic example observed by one of the writers (P.D.P.):

'Late one night a party of us arrived at a guest house in Gloucestershire. The moment I was over the threshold I knew that the house was haunted. This did not worry me in the least. I was cold and hungry, and too tired to think of anything but bed.

'As soon as I got into bed I fell asleep. A short while later I was wakened by what I thought at first was someone wandering round my room. There was no sound, but my impression was of a person stumbling about in the dark. I switched on the light and noted the time. It was one o'clock. I turned off the light again. The queer disturbance began once more. I endeavoured to find out what had wakened me, and I saw a middle-aged woman, white-faced and dark-haired, walking round and round the room in a distraught fashion. She was wringing her hands in distress, but her behaviour was curiously automatic, as though she were quite unaware of her actions. For a while I watched her, and then turned over and went to sleep.

'In the morning my friends declared they too had had a disturbed night. They had slept in the opposite corner of the house, but were wakeful and felt that the atmosphere was heavy, depressing and vaguely disturbing.

'About a year later I met a woman who told me she owned the house next to the guest house. I remarked casually that the guest house was haunted by an unhappy ghost. At this she started violently and asked what the ghost looked like. I described her with care, filling in all the details I could recall. Then she said, "That is my aunt. She owned that house and died there. She committed suicide while in a very depressed and distraught state of mind."

'We then discussed what could be done to clear up the atmosphere of the house, and liberate it from the woman with the old fixed pattern of thought. My new acquaintance was an ardent churchwoman, and she felt that a special mass and prayers would effect the change that was necessary. Be that as it may, the change did take place, and the result was that in a month or two visitors to the guest house were exclaiming at the new, light feeling in the place, and said openly that the old atmosphere of gloom had departed.'

Another example was found in a fine old manor-farm in Wiltshire. A new owner came to live in it, but was always uncomfortable because of an atmosphere of depression which hung like a cloud over one room. When the place was psychically investigated it was found that it was haunted by an elderly woman, gaunt and strange-looking, who wandered about that room in an atmosphere of deepest gloom. She seemed to have been insane with melancholia, and to have been kept there, virtually a prisoner, until she died. Since she was wrapped up in herself, the loss of the physical body made no impression on her mind, and she continued to wander vaguely about exactly as she had done in life, and she was there all the time.

On the other hand, in another old house the haunt was of an elderly man in priestly clothes, who was occasionally seen hurrying through a particular bedroom and disappearing through the wainscot into what had once been a priest-hole. Here, unlike the other, the haunt seemed to consist not of a whole human being, but of a collection of highly charged thoughts and feelings left behind and carrying out automatically a drama related to a particular event in the old priest's life. The man himself, as an ego, was not there: only some of his thoughts or 'psychons' seemed to be the actors in the haunting.

It sometimes happens that hauntings go on for centuries, while at other times one will last for a time and then clear up of its own accord. This may be due to a number of factors. One of these is the amount of intrinsic energy in the psychons left behind. A haunt highly charged with emotion or passion would probably be one which automatically persisted, while one of more neutral hue would tend to exhaust itself and die away. An earthbound soul, however, produces its own energy (which may be the force psychologists speak of as the libido) and so keeps itself going indefinitely unless something happens to make it break out of its old habits and realise that it can behave differently. This usually does happen, after some lapse of time.

There is another and rather more mysterious factor in known haunts, which is the way in which they tend to be revived or revitalised at certain times of year or under set conditions. It may be that unknown natural energies have something to do with this, much as nature sets periods of activity and of quiescence for trees and the animal kingdom.

Ghosts and Haunts

At once a further problem crops up. Does a ghost manifest, or any of the other phenomena associated with haunting, take place in the absence of an observer? That is, will a ghost show itself or make a noise if there is no human being to see or hear it? Would Hamlet's father have appeared on the battlements if Hamlet or his friends had been replaced by an automatically controlled cine-camera? The experiment, as far as we know, has not been tried. It is true that thermometers and microphones have been used in exploring haunted houses, but, it appears, they have always been within the purview of the investigators themselves.

Once more we may allow ourselves to speculate. A ghost may be perceived in one of two ways: either the observer may somehow have his paracognitive functions activated so that he perceives the 'man who isn't there'— physically at least; or else conditions are such that the psychic entity somehow succeeds in materialising so far as to produce physical sounds, or to be seen with the ordinary eye. That is, from some source or other he must gather together sufficient of that material called ectoplasm for the purpose of his ghostly manifestation. Ectoplasm is the name given to a form of cloudy material which has been seen to emerge from the body of a medium in trance. It may be so diffused as to be barely visible as a cloud of faint mist, it may condense into the form of objects or people, and it may become temporarily so firm as to be touched or to be capable of supporting heavy weights. The observer himself may be the medium from which such material is drawn. This can happen all the more easily at night, during the relaxation of sleep, and especially if, as is often the case, the person who sees the haunt is wakened in a fright.

Ghosts and Haunts

Here is an instance which occurred to one of the writers (P.D.P.): 'I was returning from Scotland by car with my secretary, but we got delayed by engine trouble, and could not reach London that night. It was very dark and neither my secretary nor I knew where we were, having missed the main road some miles back. We found ourselves in an unknown village and pulled up outside the only inn. I asked if we could have a meal and whether we could be put up for the night. The innkeeper said he could manage a scratch meal, but there were only two small rooms available, which opened into each other. These we were thankful to accept.

'During the meal I realised that this had been an old posting inn, and that it was still odd and quaint. On being shown to our rooms, I knew that the old house was haunted, and that the inner room of the two bedrooms had a much stronger atmosphere of the haunt than the outer. So I chose this room for myself because I am not usually worried by such things.

'I fell asleep immediately, only to be wakened some hours later by a sense of suffocation, feeling two hands round my neck. Opening my eyes, I saw bending over me a pale-faced man, with a mask over his eyes. He was dressed in a dark-green travelling coat and three-cornered hat, and looked in every way like the story-book highwayman. By that time I was choking and was furiously angry at what I felt to be an unwarrantable attack, so I sat up in bed and told him in no measured terms what I thought. In the usual way of ghosts when challenged in a positive spirit, he disappeared into thin air, leaving me with a bruised neck—or at least, it felt bruised though there were no marks to be seen.

'At breakfast next morning I said to the maid, "I

73

don't like your ghost, he might be dangerous to some people." She stammered an excuse and went on to say it was just imagination. I said calmly, "Don't be silly, you know perfectly well this place is haunted by a high-wayman," and she then admitted that once in a while this happened, and it often frightened people who slept in that particular room.'

Fear is a factor of great importance where haunts are concerned, especially if the ghost be of an unpleasant or malicious type. It is the fear which makes him dangerous, as distinct from merely unpleasant, and allows him to cause physical injury. If a ghostly highwayman wakes one in the middle of the night and one feels his hands on one's throat, one naturally enough expects to be strangled. Next day there may be bruises on the neck and one concludes that indeed strong material hands inflicted the injury. In reality, however, it is probable that the hands of the haunt were, at the most, sufficiently dense to be felt, while they may not have been material at all in the physical sense. But one *believed* and *expected* them to be capable of inflicting injury, and the potent malignant character of the ghost gave this belief power, so that psychic repercussion took place upon the body and marks appeared there which were out of all proportion to the physical impact which caused them.

Repercussion of this kind is an important point to understand, because it is only so that one learns to avoid it. It can be prevented if one knows the laws through which it operates and does not allow oneself to be caught unawares. It is probable that it takes place on the principle of resonance from the psychic to the physical level, in the way that harmonics are produced by sound.

If a note in music be sounded, there are a whole series

of other notes related to it. If any object such as a glass tumbler should, when struck, give as its note one of the harmonics of the original note, then, when the first note is struck again, that tumbler will be set in vibration too, giving out its own particular sound. Harmonics may be above or below the note struck.

If a ghost appears to be gripping his victim's throat, it is, as we said, unlikely that his hands will be material enough to do any damage. But to the victim it appears as if his physical neck were being squeezed. This belief allows the psychic event to react on the physical organism by such a process of resonance as we have outlined.

Even so, however, physical tissue damage is unlikely to result unless the original psychic impact be amplified and its energy increased. This happens through fear. Just as the weak waves reaching a radio receiver are amplified by means of the electrical energy flowing in the set, so does fear amplify the psychic impact from within the psycho-physical organism of the victim. The result may be physical injury, bruising, or even death. The point is that without both the fear and the belief that such physical damage would result, the repercussion would not take place. It is not the ghost who killed the victim, but the victim kills himself through fear.

The answer to the problem is thus simple enough—in theory. If a ghost should be a nuisance, and one treats it positively, say by getting angry with it, one may very well explode it and drive it out of existence for good and all. The great thing, in short, is to treat the majority of ghosts rather casually and not to take them too seriously, nor even to be too much interested in them, otherwise one may actually give them the energy which they need to recharge themselves and so to keep the pattern going.

Ghosts and Haunts

The ghost or haunt is an active phenomenon usually stimulated by certain conditions which tend to follow a pattern. This is quite different from those instances where a sensitive person reconstructs, from the atmosphere of a room, the kind of people and events which belonged to it in the past. The first is like looking at a drama acted by solid figures, the other is like looking at photographs or a cinematograph record. In practice, however, it is probable that the two processes, that of perceiving a haunt and that of perceiving a general atmosphere, overlap and combine to a considerable extent.

To be frank, nobody as yet knows enough about these matters to be didactic. All we can do is to suggest general principles as underlying the known phenomena.

5

SPIRITUALISM

This is a movement based on the belief in continuity of life after the death of the body. In this it is in line with most religious thought, but it goes further in stating that communication between the living and the dead can be established and maintained by the intermediary of certain people known as mediums. These are men or women of a certain temperament who, it is said, act as a go-between. They either transmit messages directly in either direction, or they temporarily abdicate the control of their own psycho-physical mechanism in favour of a discarnate human being who then delivers the messages himself. We shall discuss these claims more fully in later chapters.

In the last twenty-five years, more and more people have been drawn towards spiritualism. Many come to it because they hope to receive some kind of personal comfort, and the assurance that all is well with somebody who has died. Others seek knowledge and enlightenment, either from observation of the phenomena themselves, or because they hope for oracular teaching to come from the mouth of the medium while under the control of some dead—and hence, wise—spirit. Others again are merely curious and look for the excitement of signs and wonders which they hope will be produced for their edification. A minority seek to play the part of detectives, looking for and exposing fraud, and this is useful, though perhaps not very constructive.

Those who have lost loved relatives are naturally anxious to try to obtain some message which will not only convince them that they have not been extinguished when their bodies died, but also that they are happy, and that the love felt by those left behind is reciprocated. This desire clearly touches on a number of fundamental questions as to the nature of personality. Does it depend for its existence as an identifiable thing on the physical body? Can the discarnate man still think and feel as he could on earth? Is there any remembrance of earthly links with people and events? Or, when man dies, does some mysterious transformation take place so that he loses all his previous attributes, and either ceases altogether to exist, or becomes something godlike in his wisdom and omniscience? If this is so, should not any teaching or communication coming from him be treated with the utmost reverence and respect?

The average person who attends a séance, at any rate for the first time, hopes for a message from the dead and often seems to receive what he is looking for, and if he is given a more or less evidential communication, he usually goes away satisfied that he has, indeed, been in contact with the person he has been seeking. Usually he is told that the contact has been made possible by the benevolence and superior wisdom of a spirit guide, who is said to control the medium. That guide may also take the opportunity of giving some philosophical and ethical teaching to the sitter—often very much to the point, and of real value to him. Sometimes, too, if the sitter is a person of the right temperament, he is told that he himself is under the supervision of guides of his own, who are preparing him to take part in important work on spiritualistic lines.

All this may be entirely true. On the other hand, it may not. The trouble is that so many, both among the sitters and the mediums, are not mentally equipped to assess the probabilities, or to understand where and how differences and error are likely to arise. Too often the sitters do not *want* to have questions or doubts raised in their minds. They are so anxious that what is told them should be true, and their faith in it is founded on so frail a structure, that any sceptic is looked upon as a blasphemer of holy things, and therefore unworthy of attention.

On the other hand, there are those who constantly go to mediums and all kinds of séances, yet who cannot believe that anything they see or hear is not a put-up job. Their minds are at once avid to be convinced, yet closed against conviction, because, like the others, their outlook on life is built round such uncertain premises that they dare not allow any new or unusual concept to come into it, lest it collapse. To have to give up a mental pattern to which one has been accustomed from long usage can be a most disconcerting and uncomfortable event.

What then is the truth about all these things? Nobody can be certain, despite the dogmatic statements of certain spiritualists, and especially mediums. Long experience in psychological lore tells us that in every case there are more possibilities than one. The truth can only be reached by examining each particular instance in terms of these possibilities. Only after a careful balancing up of one against another is it likely that a swift moment of conviction and acceptance of one or the other possibilities may be reached. This conviction is a thing which lies beyond rational consideration, and is of the truly intuitive nature which in effect says, 'This to me is true; or if it is not, then I can trust nothing in my experience.'

Much of what follows may appear to be negative, and destructive of spiritualistic teaching. Moreover, it may seem to imply that mediums often act in bad faith. This is not at all what we intend. Most mediums are honest people, even though the problems of their calling demand much more study and understanding than the majority of them, or their clients, care to undertake. Furthermore, from the analysis which follows it may be thought that we deny that communications from the dead ever take place.

Far from this being our view, our own long experience of contact with both the seen and unseen worlds leaves little doubt as to the true and the illusory nature of many things in both worlds. This applies especially to matters which are communicated from one side of life to the other, through the imperfect mechanism of the human psyche. The purpose of putting these critical considerations forward is an attempt to answer some of the many questions which are constantly evoked by spiritualism and its practices. It is only by bringing long and varied knowledge of mediums and of the séance-room to the principles of modern psychological thought that any clue can be found to the apparent contradictions which are thrust upon us at every turn.

Another consideration prompts this analysis, which is the possible wishes of the 'dead' themselves. This is usually forgotten by those who are anxious to reach them for their own reassurance. One can well imagine that the person who has left his body may himself want to make contact with those he has left behind, whether out of

Spiritualism

affection for them or because he wants to give them some useful information either about worldly affairs or about his new state of being. If the dead person is intelligent, one can imagine also his distress either if his friends block any contact with him by their own self-frustrating avidity for it, or if they accept as coming from him some message which he has not sent nor wishes to send. The first case may well be as exasperating as trying to say something to somebody who will not stop talking; the latter, as when people take forged letters as genuine. No reasonable person can be satisfied with such a state of things; hence it behoves us, both for our own sakes, and for the sake of those who have, as we say 'passed over', to try and get the business straight, or at least, as straight as our present knowledge allows.

One of the most important lessons which psychology has taught us is the power of the unconscious mind to play tricks on the conscious. The unconscious mind can stand between us and the acceptance of a patent truth; it can bias our judgment so that unconscious desires will lead us to believe things obviously absurd. The literature of psycho-analysis and kindred schools is full of information about this. And even if one disagrees with his interpretation, Freud's *Psycho-pathology of Everyday Life* contains enough truth to make one scrutinise oneself in this respect.

In spiritualism, however, the unconscious mind plays a special and highly significant role, in addition to the more personal and individual effects described above. For, whether we like it or not, the sitter going to a medium takes his unconscious as well as his conscious mind with him, and the medium too is affected by that part of him which lies beyond the immediate confines of his conscious attention.

81

Spiritualism

It is, moreover, a characteristic of the human mind that no impression ever made on it is ever effaced. Thus, the fact that we have 'completely forgotten' a thing, or have 'never thought of it for years', does not mean that the forgotten thing is not to be found on some shelf in the background, where nature has carefully stored it. *Thus, anything which we have ever known or read or seen or heard can, in certain circumstances, be dug up and brought out of the limbo of unconsciousness.* As a result of repeated and constant experience and observation psychologists know this to be a fact. It is, however, insufficiently considered and appreciated by the majority of spiritualists.

Further, a memory strongly tinged with emotion is apt to be more active in the unconscious than is remembrance of a dry intellectual fact. And if the conscious mind has been much concerned about a thing, associated memories and feelings in the unconscious are inclined to be stirred into special and vivid activity, even though they may not again become conscious. For instance, if a person has died, all kinds of associations and memories connected with that person—what some schools of psychology call a complex of thoughts and feelings—will probably be roused in the unconscious mind, even if they stay there and do not necessarily appear in the field of awareness at all.

Curiously enough, the memories in the unconscious are more likely to be tapped by a medium than are those of which the sitter is himself aware at the time of the sitting. The reason for this is not difficult to find. The clear, active mind holds thoughts tightly. There is a kind of tension in it which keeps it stretched like a piece of well-woven fabric, so that it is not easy to pick out a single thread and unravel it from the rest. If there is something in the mind of the medium which is akin to a particular thought then the rapport is easier. If the sitter is especially self-contained and aloof, rapport remains difficult. On the other hand, conscious thought *can* be projected out of the individual field, and deliberately thrown into the common pool of a group or circle. It may then become more powerful than the inchoate unconscious material in that group and—as will be shown in a later chapter—it can then influence the whole picture which emerges. But, for the most part, people do not so project their conscious thoughts, but keep them gathered around themselves within the guardian wall of their own ego.

In contrast to this, the unconscious does not present the same obstacles. The facts and images released from the clear focus of consciousness are no longer gripped by its tension, and so are more free. The conscious field is like the rock to which seaweed is attached, the unconscious like the water in which its leaves and fringes float loose. It seems to be much easier for a medium to contact and absorb the feelings of the loose thoughts than of those which are firmly bound to earth.

Another important characteristic of the unconscious mind is that it is a field where desire and not objective thinking predominates. The ideas in it are formed round the wishes of the thinker. It is essentially the realm to which the hackneyed phrase 'wishful thinking' applies. If a person wants something to happen, but consciously says to himself 'Don't be silly! It can't and won't happen', and dismisses the idea, the wish still remains; but it is now in the unconscious rather than the conscious field, and has the freedom which results from being dismissed from the orderly class-room of deliberate thought. The same may be the case if, let us say, a person goes to a medium without any conscious desire except to examine the phenomena occurring. The medium may suddenly produce personal material relating to the student, tapping his unconscious mind and bringing to light hopes and desires of which perhaps he himself may be quite unaware, and interpret them as things about to be fulfilled.

For instance, a business man whose whole outward life has been devoted to industry may be told that he is being trained by guides to become a great musician. He may be inclined to take the idea seriously, yet as the years go on, nothing comes of it. If he takes the trouble to examine his life carefully, he may find that, as a boy, he wished to be a musician. As he grew up he forgot the wish—or rather, stifled it. But it remained, buried in his mind, but by no means dead, until resuscitated and interpreted by the medium in terms which would appeal to her client.

All these things need to be remembered when we come to study the phenomena of the séance room. Not only will the unobjective enquirer find his judgment warped by his desires, so that he accepts uncritically things which appeal to his emotions rather than to his reason, but even the seemingly detached person, brought face to face with personal material taken from his own unconscious but none-the-less personal mind, may be much startled by the way in which he is personally touched by it. Then he, too, may lose his objectivity, and find himself deceived as to the nature of what he is told.

These facts also help to explain why a person anxious to get in touch with a dead relative often fails entirely to get any comfort from mediums, until he is on the point of giving up the search as hopeless. Then, suddenly he is rewarded by a flood of supposed communications from his relative. The reason for this *may*, of course, be that at

long last the dead person has been able to break through
the barriers which prevented him from getting in touch
sooner. It may also be that the enquirer, while he was
feverishly and desperately demanding such communication, was holding the idea fast in his conscious mind,
and so out of reach of the medium. When he relaxes the
intensity of the search, and dismisses it from the field of
possibility, then the wish can float free in his unconscious,
ready to be tapped by the next medium he happens to
meet; and it is often produced for him in a casual and
unexpected way, which makes it all the more surprising,
and hence seemingly valid.

Here is a case in point. 'An intelligent man had recently
lost his only daughter. She was an exceptionally gifted
and brilliant girl, who had died after a long illness, at
the age of nineteen. The father had been going to one
medium after another, trying to get into touch with her,
and had had no success. Finally he came to me, both to
discuss his failure, and to ask if he could not find some
better line of approach.

'I began by suggesting that he was probably frustrating
himself by *demanding* of life that things should be otherwise than they were. I said that I thought the best
course would be to make an inner act of acceptance of
the physical loss of his daughter, coupled with a realisation
that life had mysterious purposes of its own, far beyond
human reason. Such an act of faith—provided it was
real and felt from the heart—would be far more likely to
lead him to an intuitive sense that the link with his
daughter was unbroken, save at the physical level. Even
though he might not receive verbal messages of unproven
authenticity, he might derive a much greater sense of
satisfaction than any outer manifestations would give.

Spiritualism

'During this conversation, I heard my wife return from a shopping expedition. I wanted to introduce her to my visitor, for reasons quite different from the purpose of his visit. I went to find her and discovered her shelling peas in the kitchen. She said she would come as soon as she had finished an urgent telephone call, which she did a few minutes later. After introductions had been made I said, "Mr. C. has called because he has lost his daughter and wants very much to get into touch with her".

' "Don't tell me any more," interrupted my wife. She turned to the visitor.

' "This may very well be pure nonsense, but I tell you it for what it is worth. Was her name Margery, and was she nineteen when she died, and had she been ill for a long time?"

'She then described Margery, her features, temperament, and outstanding capacities. She went on to say that while she was shelling peas before being fetched, a young girl suddenly appeared psychically and said, "I am Margery. Please tell my Daddy that I am trying to do what he wants. But he will not find me through séances. I want to communicate directly with him. Tell him not to be so impatient, but to go on trying to find me, even though it takes some time. Give him my love and tell him not to *think* too much, but to try and *feel* me."

'The father exclaimed, "That is what I wanted more than anything else. It has given me confidence to go on my own way, and not to listen to what other people tell me." '

This incident as between a father, his dead daughter, and a third person unknown to either, can, of course, be interpreted by the sceptic as an elaborate telepathic hallucination. In that case it would scarcely have conveyed to the outside person the sense of vivid and vital personality which the apparition gave, and seems much more likely to have been a real visit from a dead person who had been trying to find the right channel through which to put a message—like a person trying to find the right telephone number, but finding it difficult to get through because of confusion in the exchange: the exchange being previously to this a mixture of her father's and the medium's minds on which, so far, Margery had been able to make no impression.

The interpretation of this particular episode seems to lean rather in the direction of its being what it purported to be, that is, veridical touch from a dead person, alive and rational though out of the body, who found an adequate channel—through a trained psychic working in full consciousness, and not through a medium in trance—to send a message to her father. Other explanations there may be, and these should be borne in mind. In any case, it has a bearing on two major issues which need to be discussed. One is the source of the information provided by mediums. Another is why confusion and error are apt to occur. It relates, too, to the whole problem of survival which has already been set out.

POSTSCRIPT TO THIS CHAPTER, BY P.D.P.

While writing this book it occurred to me that I was not personally familiar with present-day trance work. It being quite fifteen years since I attended any sort of séance, it seemed only fair and reasonable to make a new estimate of such work. Accordingly, I arranged a number of séances for myself. From them I discovered that there was no difference at all between the work of to-day and that of twenty years ago.

Spiritualism

There were certain general characteristics which applied to each medium I visited, the first was that each séance began with the medium going under a supposed control, but after ten minutes or so had elapsed, each medium reverted to her own personality, without being in the least aware of it. I noticed particularly that each control made the same grammatical errors, or had the same tricks of speech as the medium; that each control and medium used a lot of automatic phrases which were repeated frequently; and that when passing on messages presumably from dead people, these idiosyncracies persisted.

‘ Secondly, each séance began with the medium giving descriptions and names of people of whom I had never heard or seen. When there was no recognition on my part they abandoned the effort. But this preliminary opening seemed to serve a purpose, like a tuning-in process. It was as though the medium was fumbling around to discover the right key, or strike the correct note.

The third thing which interested me was that, at some point in this feeling around, the medium suddenly tapped something in myself. To me, in each case, it appeared to be my mind with which she made a contact. It was like tuning a wireless receiver to a particular station. To my clairvoyant sight a small light suddenly glowed in the aura over the medium's head.

After this contact had been established, there seemed no difficulty for the medium. There was a flow of description, rather generalised, but quite correct, yet nothing was introduced which was not already well known to me.

At one séance a striking fact was that as my mind associated a number of memories and feelings with the material presented, the medium invariably gave these back to me about half a minute later. It was as though she were on my mental track, and as I thought a thing, she seemed to respond to that thought, and then echo it as though she had received it from 'the other side'.

Later in that séance I was distinctly aware of another factor being introduced, and to my own perception this was a genuine element of telepathy from the mind of a person out of the body. My own thoughts and feelings were no longer the dominant part of the work. The medium went on quite steadily, and acted as a bridge, over which travelled the mental messages, but she was obviously unaware of any difference between my mind and the mind of the communicator. It bore out entirely the theory that the mind in a living person and the mind of a dead person operate in the same way. I summed that particular séance up as a very good demonstration of telepathy both from this side of death and the other.

At another sitting with another medium, the whole of the material of this first séance was repeated, just like a gramophone record being played. I sat wondering how long it would keep its sequence and where it would differ from the first, but to my astonishment, the whole proceeding was followed from beginning to end, just as it had happened the first time. Obviously, to me, this was only a telepathic reading of my own mind, because this time there was no atmosphere or any other feeling of any dead person being present.

During these experimental séances, if I was unknown to the medium, I escaped without a lot of flattery, but in one or two instances, where the medium gave away the fact that she knew who I was, I was regaled with a lot of very tedious and rather stupid eulogy. People who have been to many séances will appreciate the common-place pattern of all this.

6

THE NATURE OF MEDIUMSHIP

It will be well to explain once more what exactly is meant by mediumship. To do this adequately, it is imperative to know something about psychological principles, as well as the basic facts about mediumship itself. The term is popularly used to imply the ability to transmit to the physical brain consciousness something of one's psychic perception. In this sense, it covers everybody who is psychically perceptive, but since this applies to some extent to every one of us, whether we know it or not, it is better to reserve the word for a psychic person who is said to be able to transmit communications from the dead. This means that he must be receptive on the one hand to the life of the invisible world, and, on the other hand, able to transmit his experience in some physically demonstrable form. He may be in the position to control and direct his own phenomena, or if not, he abdicates for the time being in favour of some form of 'control', who manipulates the medium's mechanism and uses it temporarily as a means of expressing himself directly. Here we immediately land into difficulty, because there are several other explanations of mediumistic phenomena.

The Nature of Mediumship

One of the discoveries made by psychiatrists is that there are different forms of mental, as of physical, disease. We have learned how to differentiate a case of measles from scarlet fever or pneumonia. Once the diagnosis is made one can forecast the probable course of the illness. It is the same with the sicknesses of the mind. We know that an acute outburst of mania will probably subside quickly, but may recur, while a paranoiac is never likely to lose his ideas of persecution or his megalomania. But in mental illness there is something more, for it is found that it develops according to a certain pattern which can be traced back to its beginning. That is to say, *dementia praecox* will only grow from a root which is its own, while mania or melancholia belong to another category, and the person afflicted with that disease could not, in the nature of things, become a victim to *dementia praecox*.

In other words, a rather rough and ready classification exists for certain temperaments which, if they should become mentally unbalanced—and, as we know, not one in a thousand can be labelled insane—will develop along a certain line and no other. We thus speak of the *schizoid* type, the *cyclothymic*, the *obsessional*, or the *hysteric*, applying these labels to people, most of whom are not in the least abnormal, nor likely to become so. It is like labelling people by the pattern of their skulls, as dolicho-cephalic (or long-skulled), brachycephalic (or short-skulled) and so on. The label refers to a type, not to a disease.

The assessment of mental types is not easy, and in practice very few people run true to form. Most of us are a mixture, perhaps with one pattern outstanding, or with a fundamental type obscured by an overlay of an-other. The reasons for such an overlay are too technical for anything but a psychiatric textbook, but the principle is worth bearing in mind.

The point is that, if one makes an abstraction of all the characteristics belonging to one particular type, these make up a picture or pattern of that type, similar to the composite photographs which anthropologists sometimes use in the analysis of racial characteristics. They represent what is common to all members of that race, yet every individual differs from the composite picture in some way. Thus, every human being can, if one wishes, be given the label of one type or another, according to his predominant characteristics.

If, therefore, one places mediumship as characteristic of the hysterical 'syndrome' or composite pattern, this is not being in the very least derogatory of the medium. Nor does it mean that anyone acting as a medium is necessarily a hysteric; he may be a schizoid type, for instance, with an overlay of hysterical characteristics. Still less does it mean that the medium is likely to have uncontrolled bouts of emotion, or any of the characteristics commonly associated with hysteria. What it does mean, however, is that he has the ability to dissociate his personality in a particular way and at a particular level. This fact makes relevant an excursion into the psychology of the hysterical syndrome.

There are various ways in which the personality can abstract itself from clearly focused physical consciousness. We all do this when we slip into a brown study, bury ourselves in an exciting book, or go to sleep in the ordinary way. In certain forms of mental disease, also, the victim becomes so much absorbed in his own thoughts that he is inaccessible, apparently unconscious, and highly resistant to disturbance.

The Nature of Mediumship

The hysterical temperament, however, has its own ways of withdrawal. 'Ways' is in the plural, because the syndrome is highly complex and shows many aspects. The one which concerns us is that direct withdrawal of the normal consciousness of the usual personality from its usual relationship with everyday life. This complicated and repetitive phrase needs analysing.

Normal consciousness is that with which, in our usual frame of mind, we look at the world around us, and the normal personality is that immediate aspect of ourselves which does the looking round. William Smith, walking down the road or looking at the flowers in his garden in an equable frame of mind, is such a normal personality seeing life in a normal way. Suppose, however, that William Smith is a hysteric, and something happens which, in the technical phrase, dissociates him. His usual attitude to life becomes as it were dislocated and is replaced either by a new one or, in less serious cases, becomes confused and uncertain. He no longer sees the road or the flowers as he did. He may, in fact, lose sight of them altogether, while the onlooker may become aware of the fact that William is dazed, as if sleep walking. Perhaps he blunders about aimlessly, or he may even fall down in a trance. Perhaps he suddenly starts a completely new train of action, different from what he was doing before and leading to another end. He may even go a step further than this, and the body of William Smith seems to become animated and possessed by another personality with a psychology of its own, capable of acting and behaving in just as normal a way as William himself. If one investigated the new personality, one would find that he did not know his real name or anything about his history or background, or else that he would give a fictitious and imaginary account of himself. William Smith would then, perhaps, wander from home, stay at an hotel, buy what he needed, maybe go so far as to marry another woman and take another job. This might last until something happened to reverse the process and he suddenly 'came to' and remembered his identity.

William Smith is an extreme instance, but cases just as dramatic have been recorded. Many of those who are advertised for as 'probably suffering from loss of memory' are in some degree afflicted with the same trouble. Sometimes the dissociation is only momentary, a matter of a few seconds, sometimes it lasts for hours or days. Often the victim is dazed and vague, the well-defined secondary personality being a rarity. There are all grades of this condition, but in all cases the mechanism is the same. If one analyses both the cause—often a mental and emotional shock or sudden fright—and the ensuing behaviour, or, if one can, the type of personality assumed during the 'fugue', as it is called, one finds a direct psychological relationship between William Smith and his *alter ego*, the latter representing a facet of William Smith as unacceptable to him in his everyday, normal character of William, as Mr. Hyde was to Dr. Jekyll.

This is a tabloid summary of hysterical dissociation. You will find such cases much more fully discussed in psychiatric literature.[1]

If William Smith can apparently be dispossessed and replaced by someone else, in what way is he different from a medium under control? First, William is a sick man, in whom dissociation is a symptom of the disease. The medium is not. William is dissociated willy-nilly, when

[1] See, for instance, Henderson and Gillespie, *A Text-book of Psychiatry*.

submitted to certain emotional or physical strains and stresses. The medium, in principle, and after training, dissociates only at will. What both William and the medium have in common is a certain type of psychic personality which allows of easy dissociation, just as there are people exceptionally flexible in body and therefore said to be double-jointed. In spiritualism it has always been accepted that the mediumistic capacity is a special and superior quality, and mediums are usually spoken of as being specially gifted. If William's hysteria were turned into a constructive channel, he would be as mediumistic as anyone else. This statement of the case will not be acceptable to certain people; but our experience both of personal mediumship and of psychological medicine have made this increasingly clear to us.

Another characteristic of mediumship is that, in order that his paracognitive, or 'psychic' faculty shall function, the medium undergoes some form of deliberate loosening of the physical consciousness, which varies from the slightest degree of drowsiness to complete and deep trance. In other words, the medium works under conditions where voluntary control of himself and awareness of the physical surroundings are diminished. This is clearly a very different thing from the way of the really well-trained psychic seer, who is capable of functioning in full physical consciousness, or even in a state of enhanced awareness of both his material and his psychic environment.

Hence, it will probably be best if we restrict the use of the term medium to people who, in order to reach a wider field of perception from their normal physical consciousness, have to dissociate or weaken their hold temporarily on physical life. This dissociation, as we have suggested, may happen spontaneously. In such a case the medium needs to be taught to make the occurrence deliberate and controlled, instead of erratic and involuntary. On the other hand, there are others, the majority in fact, whose training in 'development' circles is directed towards learning *how* to bring about dissociation, or the trance condition. They are taught deliberately to slip into a 'half-way state' which is, strictly speaking, a condition of slight self-hypnosis, wherein the mediumistic person loses clear-cut perception of his environment, which seems to recede to the far end of a tunnel. It has been described by some as similar to looking down the wrong end of a telescope, when everything may be very clear but also very small and remote. Some mediums never progress beyond a vague and inchoate state of consciousness, of which the most apt description is that of a balloon floating among the clouds on the end of a long cable. The work of these, like themselves, is generally vague and ill-defined. Their experience of the half-way state, too, is probably less like that of the remote, clear field, than of the physical world becoming blurred and colourless and replaced by a mass of drifting cloud in which occur occasional glimpses of physical forms, symbolic shapes, or scenes either of this world or the psychic world. This kind of mediumistic work lends itself to much distortion and even exaggeration, the medium finding it difficult to place his material and even more unable to intercept correctly what he sees or feels.

There is thus a distinction between the positive and negative forms of psychism or paracognition, the medium being the one who functions on the negative side and in a dissociated condition, whether in the séance room or out of it. They are mostly persons whose psychic capacity is primitive, often quite involuntary, governing rather than serving them. There is also a large group of people

The Nature of Mediumship

with partially developed psychic faculties, which they usually try to expand by various methods. The main method in spiritualism is sitting quietly, either with a group, a chosen friend or a member of the family, and allowing the 'guide', whether an extraneous individual or another aspect of their own personality, to control them and pursue whatever line of interest the controlling entity desires. Practically always, there is little, if any, knowledge of the rationale of the subject. The involuntary or negative psychic responds to ordinary life and psychic experience chiefly through his sympathetic nervous system. He is often painfully over-sensitised and affected by his surroundings, to which his reactions are almost entirely emotional.

Only those people can be called positive psychics whose capacities are under the control of their own will. They use their cerebro-spinal system and are able to analyse the impacts on it, and, if necessary, can refuse to respond to them. They are keenly sensitive to a wide range of impressions, plus an intuitive, as well as psychic, perception of their meaning, and their work brings with it a sense of conviction. The difference between the two types is like that between a child who eats anything offered in the way of food, and a food expert who selects his nourishment in terms of values such as vitamins and calories. Further, the positive psychic does not produce spontaneous physical phenomena such as raps, apports or table-lifting, which still sometimes happen with mediums, though much less commonly, it would seem, than heretofore, when civilised life and consequently the mental alertness of many was much lower than it is to-day.

If we include physical phenomena in our list of mediumistic attributes, this will enable us to classify mediumship as lying between the two extremes of the poltergeist medium,[1] who is usually entirely unaware of any change in himself during the phenomena, through the range of mediums who use unconscious self-hypnosis, and that of the large majority who function in a deliberately induced semi-conscious state, to those rare ones who become completely dissociated and unconscious in full trance.

Poltergeist mediums are usually and characteristically primitive, uneducated, young people, sometimes an adolescent girl or boy of low-grade intelligence. The key to their mediumship is a certain looseness of texture in their psychological make-up which enables them to carry on normal activities while being the agents through which the phenomena occur. Thus a maid-servant may be washing the dishes in quite a natural way when in another room of the house the furniture may move about, or solid objects be flung through the air. It is obvious that in this, as in other physical phenomena, *work* in the scientific sense is being done, and hence *energy* is required and used up in doing that work. The medium appears to be the battery from which the energy is derived, but without disturbance of consciousness. It is evident, of course, that the same scientific principle must apply to all genuine physical phenomena, whether these be merely raps or whether they involve movement of heavy objects, apports, or materialisations. But in most cases the medium is not busy on routine work while the phenomena take place.

The medium who goes spontaneously into trance without volition is fundamentally a psychological case. This is

[1] We are not here concerned with the evidence either for poltergeists or physical phenomena. That they *do* take place is pretty well proved. But even assuming that out of a hundred cases investigated only one is genuine, the machinery of that one case needs explanation.

The Nature of Mediumship

generally not a genuine trance condition at all, but a half-way state which is not convincing to any one who is conversant with psychical research or is a good student of spiritualism. These people are a trouble in all spiritualistic societies, because, in season and out, they fall into an apparent trance condition, without any consideration for the work which may be going on and for the other people concerned. Having worked for years in one of the best known centres for spiritualistic work, the writer knows this fact only too well, having had the job of persuading this kind of mediumistic caller that it was neither the time nor the place for such demonstrations. They are, in short, much more interested in themselves than they are in any serious study. Naturally the material they produce is usually chaotic and of no value, and, as they are generally averse to any form of discipline, they cannot be trained to make proper use of what capacities they have.

The greater proportion of mediums fall under the category of those who work in semi-trance, complete trance being very rare. This is well shown by the fact that, although, most mediums believe themselves to be completely unconscious, and that they have no knowledge of anything which transpires while they are 'under control', yet, if one is in close and ordinary touch with them, one soon discovers that a great deal of what took place reappears casually in the course of conversation. If taken off their guard they will often display detailed knowledge of all that happened during their trance work. This was learnt without any shadow of doubt during the years spent each day of the week dealing with mediums, their sitters and their work.

This does not mean there is any deliberate attempt to

deceive, far from it. But awareness of what has taken place during a séance is—if we except fraud—definitely under the surface, but only just under, so that when conditions change again it tends to float up into consciousness. But—like a dream when one tries to recapture it—the chances are that any willed attempt to remember what went on would be quite enough to drive it once more out of sight.

The rare, full trance condition produces a state of unconsciousness as complete as that of deep anaesthesia, in that on returning to normal there is neither the memory nor the power to remember what took place during the trance. The difference is that no drugs are used to produce unconsciousness, and that the physical mechanism remains in full possession of its function, in so far as it can walk about the room and move in a perfectly co-ordinated manner. The normal consciousness of the medium is entirely dissociated from its mechanism, but evidently something intelligent is in control. This can show itself in a complete temporary change of personality in the medium or it may be that the controlling intelligence is more remote and manipulates the body as if it were a skilful puppet-master without actually taking possession of it.

7

THE SÉANCE OR SPIRITUALISTIC CIRCLE

Whether we are considering a private sitting of one or two people with a medium, or a circle consisting of a greater number, the psychic mechanics are very much the same, and, if we are to understand them they need to be looked at in terms of group psychology. As we have already said, we cannot, from a scientific angle, be certain whether the psyche is pure abstraction, or whether it is a quasi-material object with a shape and structure which can be expressed in physical terms. In any case, to the clairvoyant it presents itself as such an object, and whether we consider this to be merely symbolic or whether it is really an object is a theoretical point. The objective view is the more convenient, and gives us the easiest—if not in an absolute sense the truest—way of discussing its behaviour.

Most clairvoyants tell us that they see each person surrounded by a luminous cloud or aura, extending usually some two or three feet beyond the confines of the body. This is analogous to an electro-magnetic field, but does not register on the most sensitive physical instruments yet devised because the energy it represents is mental and emotional, not physical. Maybe it represents a higher octave of energy waves, but it is certainly something different from the range covered by phenomena known in the physical world.

This human aura has long been the subject of much discussion among psychics, and, although a lot has been written about it, in the last analysis very little is actually known. At first sight it appears to the trained clairvoyant as an oval cloud of swiftly moving multi-coloured mist. It surrounds the dense physical body and extends beyond it in all directions. It is not confined to a special shape, but is always shifting and changing as the thought and feeling of its owner changes. The quality, colours and tone-range of this aura are determined by the nature of the thought and feeling with which they are connected, so that the aura is intensely personal. It is so responsive, both to inner and outer stimuli, that it is seldom quiescent, and is always re-acting to its environment. This is an important fact to note, especially in dealing with the composite group aura which is formed between two or more persons in close proximity.

Each person enters the séance room with his psychic field or aura intact, and shaped around his own body. But when he has been sitting for some time near another, and in a receptive frame of mind, his own aura tends to lose its definite outline and to become merged into the aura of his neighbour. In this way a number of persons together, after a time, share a common aura. It is as though someone brought into the room a number of cups of liquid on a tray, then gradually emptied each cup into the tray itself.

This group aura has as its greatest common measure the united qualities of thought and feeling emanating from the members of the group. Thus, an unrecognised

102

telepathic rapport is set up, and feeling flows across this group aura without distinction as to the source from which it emerges. It is almost as though the group became enclosed in a fine film of ultra-responsive material, and through this film every faintest ripple in the atmosphere recorded itself. The medium is, generally speaking, very sensitive to this condition, and is often aware in two directions. In one direction, there is an increased perception of the inner world, so that details of thought and feeling become much clearer. To this is added a greatly enhanced range of knowledge, which is generally accredited to a guide or the person out of the body, who is said to be in communication with a member of the group. There is also a strange penetration into the sitters' thoughts and emotions, so that they lie open to the medium in a way that does not happen unless both medium and sitter are enclosed within one aura.

It sometimes happens that a sitter is more sensitive to the group aura than the medium, and is baffled and surprised by the amount of knowledge and perception that seems to flow into her from nowhere in particular. This is well-known to people who frequent the séance room. They will often say, after the group, that they knew what was coming before it found any expression, and that they were personally aware of every description or message that the medium gave.

At other times one special person willy-nilly dominates the whole proceedings. The medium is unable to do other than pick out information for that one person. Even when the sitter concerned becomes apologetic and embarrassed by the amount of attention thus aroused, the current still continues to flow in his direction. In point of fact this means that that individual has strong thoughts or desires which make a clear and definite impression on the group aura and, through it, upon the sensitive field of the medium's mind. Any person of dominant thought and feeling, whether these be conscious or unconscious is apt to throw out clear images and ideas which are much more sharply recorded on the composite aura than those of the muddled thinker, or an emotionally confused person who makes a faint impression on it. It is as if the medium were in a room full of pictures, some of which are bright and sharp, others vague and dull. His attention will naturally be drawn to those which strike him most vividly.

The group aura becomes as it were an entity in the psychic world. But although thought and emotion tend to become pooled in the way we have described, it is only a relative and temporary fusion. It is as if the individual aura lost its periphery, so that its contents melted into its neighbours, but the central core of that aura, the psychological ego, remained. Thus at the end of the séance, when the circle breaks up, each ego gathers round itself once more the material which it has put into the pool. It is as if one imagined a collection of one-celled amœbæ coming together and coalescing so that for the time being one had a large protoplasmic mass in which the nucleus of each amœba was embedded. At the end of the séance, each amœba draws its protoplasm back to itself, encloses it in the rather vague film which is the cell-wall, and departs on its own business. The person with a clear-cut positive mind reintegrates himself with his own material, and that only. But the suggestible person can pick up material from other people as well as his own, and so can go away more or less influenced by this additional material, somewhat as a sponge absorbs water. This is due to a negative attitude of mind. There are many such people

The Séance or Spiritualistic Circle

frequenting public circles and smaller séances, and in course of time they can find themselves in difficulties and may get into deep waters, because they do not realise what is happening to them. This type of person is in need of psychological help because it does not occur to him to stop negative psychic practices, even if those practices are very simple and only consist of attendance at a circle. Failing that, they may go from bad to worse, gradually becoming more confused and anxious because their own thoughts and feelings have become confused with others by psychic contamination. This can even influence physical health, and the person may become one of the baffling type of patient, whom every doctor knows to be genuinely ill, but for whose illness he can find no valid physical reason. Common symptoms, in bad cases, are constant hearing of voices, repetitions of visions and obsessional thoughts, none of which can be shut out. Unfortunately, the unimaginative physician, in such cases, has no better idea of treatment than to give his patient the universal panacea of to-day, phenobarbitone. This, though it may to some extent mask the insomnia and the anxiety, is, by the very nature of the patient's negative condition, likely to cause further and deeper deterioration. Some doctors are wise enough to send this sort of patient to a psychologist, and he in his turn is likely to be frustrated because he may trace the immediate cause of the trouble to attending séances, and equally rightly may discover that the deeper root comes from earlier predisposition, but he is not in a position to perceive or assess the amount of psychic contagion which has taken place. The difficulty is that so often the sufferer cannot get right until he has cleared his aura of the extraneous material. These patients often have the idea that they are possessed by a discarnate spirit. This is not so at all, but the obsession is real in so far as they have allowed thought-material from other people to trespass into their own personal field. The cure, in general terms, lies in discontinuing all negative psychic practices such as sittings, automatic writing, planchette, or even fortune-telling for amusement, as well as in trying to find a positive psychological integration.

The fact that slight remnants of differentiation persist in the circle after it has 'grouped' is one of the reasons why a medium will often ask friendly and emotionally warm people to sit next to her, rather than the intellectuals. For when she is under any degree of trance, her waking consciousness loses its defences, and makes her much more vulnerable to mass impacts from the conglomerate aura around her. For instance, an impatient thought of criticism from a sitter, if directed straight to the medium, will act exactly like a sharp instrument striking her. It can produce real shock and pain. On the other hand, criticism alone will not be detrimental, provided it is not used destructively and with an emotional drive propelling it. Very few people realise that a hypersensitive medium is often hurt more by the emotion behind a thought than by the thought itself.

Like any other psychological group, the aura in a circle represents the aggregation of the minds of those present. The unconscious as well as the conscious minds of the sitters play into it, so that the *quality* of that aura is determined by all those present, as well as by their common motive in coming together. Returning to the analogy of the cups of liquid, it is as if one were to pour cups of salt water of varying strength into the tray. The result would be a solution of strength proportionate to the amount of strong, medium, or weak solution poured in. Consequently also, the nature of the group will depend on the kinds of chemicals which are put in. Some of them will combine and mix happily, whereas others will tend to effervesce, or to become hot and explosive. Others may refuse altogether to mix, and hence, as the experienced sitter knows, the circle does not function at all.

Once more, however, physical analogies are not perfect because the aura of the group is highly labile and suggestible—that is, sensitive to every change of atmosphere. As has been pointed out, the common purpose in coming together is an important factor. Therefore, a group of sober students is more likely to produce worth-while material, than another of frivolous or highly emotional and uncritical folk who are only anxious to be reassured and comforted. These will form a circle of quite a different nature. Any group aura is highly influenced by strong thought among its members, and not only by outside influences which may come into it. This idea is not likely to appeal to those who wish to believe that there is an inner spiritual guidance at the back of it. This was proved by one of the writers (P.D.P.) who, to the dismay of some of the intelligent members of her circle, used to predict what would happen during the evening's work. She discovered that while sitting with an experimental circle of twelve to fifteen people, whose purpose was to try to help the medium to develop 'direct voice' phenomena, that is, an attempt to reproduce the actual voice of the communicator, a thing far more difficult than the usual method of communication, which takes place in the medium's own intonation.

The group itself was an interesting one. It consisted of engineers, civil servants, an architect, a doctor, and professional men and women. They were a purely experimental group, and interested in the rationale and mechanics of psychism. The writer accidentally discovered that, when she got tired of the uninteresting generalities of the medium, she could make something happen by thinking it. She would for instance focus on one member of the group and imagine some special incident connected with that person, such as the death of an elderly man of a particular appearance. Almost immediately a message or description would be given that was a duplicate of the thought she had constructed. She pointed this fact out tentatively first to an engineer, and later to other members of the group. They discussed the matter and tried simple experiments, which confirmed that the communication could be influenced in one direction or another. It was like tilting a table, or swinging a compass in any given direction. The medium was entirely ignorant that this discussion had arisen, and the other members of the group were, at first, quite sceptical about the whole thing. But one evening before the group met, this investigator told the engineer there would be a visit that evening from the entirely fictitious fiancée he had never possessed. Surely enough, during the evening, the man was addressed through or by the medium, by a young woman, telling him she was with him in death as in life, that she still loved him and was guiding and looking after him from the spirit world— in short, all the usual things which one might expect in such a case. Gradually, it became clear, in that group at any rate, that a strongly projected thought produced commensurate results. It was all very dismaying, because no one had any clue to the problem, and no one, at that time, possessed any psychological knowledge. It was such a blow to the group that they decided to abandon the experiments.

The Séance or Spiritualistic Circle

Needless to say, this was not done out of malice or mischief, nor with the slightest ill-feeling towards the medium, but in the spirit of investigation, which was the alleged purpose of the organisation which ran the circle. But—and unfortunately experienced investigators will know this is only too common—when the head of the organisation was told about the experiments, instead of accepting them in a scientific spirit, he was very angry. To be unwilling to face facts of this order is one of the reasons for the continuing confusion among *bona fide* spiritualists.

One more factor needs to be taken into account, in spiritualistic circles as in other groups—and here again the analogy of the cups of water is incomplete. For, when we are dealing with living organisms, the result of integration into a greater group is not merely a sum of the parts. It is something more, as if the group itself acquired a temporary nuclear ego round which it focused and revolved, as planets do round the sun.

This focus must, in the nature of things, be connected with the purpose of the group. Where people meet together to try and make contact with the so-called dead, the focus will, from the point of view of the living, go half-way towards making that contact possible, provided they do not ruin everything by being more interested in themselves than in the actual dead person. So that, assuming the dead can and want to communicate with the living, they, too, have to do only half the work required to build the bridge which makes such communication possible. From the point of view of the dead, therefore, one can postulate that the sensitive group aura may be a valuable and easy instrument or magnetic field for them to influence. For, if they themselves are living, bodiless, yet with their

109

psychological equipment intact, the field of the circle, belonging as it does to the same level of the universe as that where they are themselves living, is obviously suitable for them to influence from their side.

That does not mean at all that every control or alleged communicator is in fact a dead person come back for that purpose. There are, as we have already suggested, very many possibilities of error and self-deception; and, without shutting any door to the reality of such communication, it is these we must now consider.

8

GUIDES

For serious students of psychical research the possibility of getting into touch with the so-called dead
is important. They are not so much concerned with
finding an anodyne for personal grief as with seeking the
straight line of truth. Hence, it is as important to consider all possible sources of error, as it is to be willing to
admit the truth once it is found.

The commonest way of attempting to obtain such contact is through the offices of some sort of medium. Sometimes it is the relative of the dead person who is the
medium, learning how to do automatic writing or to work
a planchette. More usually the relative goes to a professional, who purports to bring that dead person into
the presence of the enquirer, or passes on a message supposed to come from him. In either case one is dealing with
the same basic psychological situation. But in the first
instance the relative of the dead person is presumed to be
directly used by him to write or spell out the messages in
characteristic language, whereas in the second case two
other people, the medium and the 'guide', make the
connecting link. That is, in the first case there is no
intermediary between the dead person and the living

Guides

relative, but in the second case the two are said to be brought into contact only through such intermediaries. These are the medium herself in the physical world, and, one is told, the medium's 'spirit guide' on 'the other side'.

The guide is an important factor, as he is said to be the active agent in bringing the dead person forward and putting him in touch with the living, through the mechanism provided by his pupil, the medium in the flesh. It is the nature of this guide which we need to understand.

As is well-known, the usual procedure of a medium with a sitter or a circle is that the medium goes into trance. It then seems as if his own personality steps aside, another moves in and is said to be that of a spirit guide. Often there is not only one guide but several, all of whom are said to be directing and teaching the medium from the other world. These guides are fairly constant attendants at séances, and they often have quite definite and recognisable personalities of their own. It is as if a student at school or in a university were taught different subjects by different teachers. They all have this in common, however, that they are thought to be superior to the ordinary person, and that they are looked up to and loved by the medium.

At times the guides announce themselves by name. At other times the medium, just before, or just as she is slipping into trance, will say something like 'Golden Hawk wants to speak to you'. The guide may tell you who he is and something of his alleged history. He may then talk to a sitter personally for a while, or launch into a dissertation which may be anything from excellent philosophy and ethics to moral clichés and platitudes. He may even predict certain things, ranging from obvious events, which can scarcely fail to happen, to great things which are supposedly about to be discovered, these, nevertheless, perhaps having their origin in Atlantis. Sometimes all that comes is merely a farrago of scarcely intelligible nonsense. All this is quite often interpolated between messages and descriptions, more or less accurate, which are said to be conveyed from the other side.

At one point the guide may relinquish his control to allow a dead person to take direct charge in his stead and to speak through the medium. This, at least, is the general method of procedure, and roughly the interpretation given.

To be able to assess this material further, dissection and scrutiny are necessary. First, what is the nature of the guide? It must be remembered that everybody has in himself some degree of the dramatic instinct. In some people this is manifest and accepted, and they quite consciously and light-heartedly enjoy 'making an entrance' or otherwise impressing people. But in others the dramatisation is less obvious and more serious because it represents a psychological need, a compensation for a feeling of inadequacy or inferiority. In others, again, the dramatic instinct is more or less repressed and dissociated, showing itself in unconscious behaviour which may result in their making scenes or having alleged fainting attacks in public, telling pathological lies, and inventing fantastic stories about themselves and what they and others are doing or have done.

Further, there are some people who have vivid imaginations, capable of generating and projecting outside themselves characters which they have themselves created and who, they may tell you, tend to come alive and go their own way. Of such people are novelists and dramatists made, and they often say that once a piece of work is under way their characters refuse to follow the lines of the plot the author has already outlined and force him to modify it. These characters have thus acquired a life and form of their own. They are in this sense independent beings who impress their wishes on their creator, much as an ordinary person can do.

There are thus several possibilities as to the real identity of the guide. One is that he is actually what he gives himself out to be: that is, a wise dead person, who is using the medium as a channel for instructing those who are still in the flesh. But, in view of the possibilities arising from the psychological temperament of which mediums are made, one must also discuss the alternatives which are often highly suggestive and significant—all the more so because a characteristic of many guides is that they are said either to be people whom the medium very much admired, or to be connected with a historical period which interests the medium, and has perhaps captured his imagination. Similarly, there are cases where the guide represents something the very opposite of what the medium is in everyday life. For instance, an ineffective and rather feeble little sempstress, felt herself to be under the influence of Oliver Cromwell.

It is natural, in these circumstances, for a deep student of Christianity to think that Archdeacon Wilberforce is her guide, or for a person steeped in ideas about ancient Egypt to be under the tutelage of a High Priest of Ra. Another, interested in healing, may be inspired by a learned physician from mediæval Florence, or—in the mistaken belief that the 'doctor' of a tribe meant a physician—by a Red Indian doctor. The guide is always looked upon as somebody of greater spiritual stature than the medium himself, and therefore as somebody to be treated with reverence and respect. But there is in this very fact a more or less unrecognised flattery of the medium. Even if the guide does not, as he so often does, extol to the circle the excellence of his pupil, there is at any rate the tacit suggestion that the medium himself has been chosen by the guide as a person of exceptional ability and attainments, no matter how mediocre his outward appearance and station in life may be.

The student of psychology will not need to have his attention drawn to the compensatory aspects of this interpretation of guidance. Whately Carington, famous as a psychical researcher, carried out psychological tests on mediums, both in trance and under the control of their guides. He found that careful analysis and correlation of these tests showed them to be complementary. This pointed strongly to the medium and the guide being only different aspects of one and the same personality, the latter being nothing more than a product from the unconscious mind of the medium.

This fact must not be taken as ruling out the possibility that the traditional view is true. It does, however, show it to be less likely. If the medium really admires some historical character, that person *may* have his attention caught by telepathic means wherever he may be in the after-death worlds. And if people in the flesh are often interested in and helpful to others, there is no reason why they should not go on feeling kindly disposed towards others, even though they have left their bodies. But the difficulty of finding positive evidence of this is very great. And, indeed, we may be permitted to suggest that such help can be better given by the discarnate through less clumsy methods than having to control a body which is not one's own. It would be easier to do this by telepathy from the mind of the one out of the body, directly to the mind of the living person. It often happens that a lecturer or a writer seems to tap some source of knowledge which does not appear to be his own, and which gives added life and power to what he is doing. This may mean either that he is opening up some level of his own psyche of which he has been completely unconscious; or it may mean that he is being inspired and fed by some other person's mind. Or, of course, it may be that both these processes are happening together.

There is another aspect of the matter. It is often easier for a sensitive to be unselfconscious if he is not directly faced by the one to whom he is talking. A shy person sometimes prefers to write a letter rather than say something directly, while the telephone serves the same purpose of avoiding a face to face encounter. A dancer once said that she felt it much easier to let herself go emotionally when she was wearing a mask than when her face could be seen by the audience. Similarly, a writer will sometimes feel that he can show up a social problem more pointedly in a play or story than he could by a straight essay. An actor will sometimes reveal his inmost feelings best while acting a particular part, and not while being his normal self. The guide can similarly act as a buffer between the personality of the medium and those he is talking to, and, as those who frequent séances will know, a guide is sometimes far more directly critical of a sitter than the medium would ever dare to be. Mediums shrink from disapproval, but under the shield of a guide it is often quite possible to get home truths which will be accepted under this guise, but would be sure to arouse resentment under the other.

A thing which bears out this point will doubtless have been noted by a number of careful observers, which is that many séances start rather stiffly, under the aegis of a guide personality, with the medium's characteristics carefully veiled. But after a time, as the atmosphere becomes easier, and the séance is in full swing, the guide appears to fade away, and bit by bit the voice and phraseology of the medium in her normal state return. It appears as if the medium has forgotten to play the part which represents the authoritative character of the guide, and goes on as her usual self, without realising what she has done. This, of course, is not trickery but a quite unconscious happening.

Thus the guide may well be a dramatic representation of a more remote part of the medium's psyche, though one unsuspected by the medium himself. He can also be a dramatised form of a part of the medium which gets no outlet, such as the romantic or adventurous part of him. He can equally represent a form of escapism by which he runs away from reality.

But, once more, there is another and more positive side to the matter—and one, which properly understood, can be of real value, if only to the medium himself. For it happens at times that the guide, even if we assume him to be only another aspect of the medium's mind, really does represent a higher and finer aspect of that mind: that is, a part with perceptions and understanding of life too deep for the timid and inhibited consciousness of the medium to allow into the light of ordinary day. He may, thus, really be a guide; but his origin lies in the subjective mind of the medium, and represents, in a symbolic image, something of the spiritual—as distinct from the merely mental or psychic—aspect of the medium himself. We quite appreciate how difficult this suggestion will be to many, but again it is born out of many years of study and experience. It is also in tune

Guides

with C. G. Jung's principle regarding archetypal figures already mentioned in Chapter 1. This is too intricate a subject to go into here, save to point out that in dreams and visions the deeper and wider self of the dreamer often shows itself as a wise old man, a sybilline woman, and the like. The 'guide' may well be simply one of these archetypal figures—truly wise, but representing the intrinsic wisdom of the medium himself, not that of some detached being.

One of the writers, during the early years of her experience, did a great deal of what seemed to all onlookers to be trance work. But she always felt this was a mistake, because she was clearly aware and conscious under the overclothing of another personality. She felt as though she were dual, thinking clearly in commonplace ways, and at the same time carrying on another line of thought and behaviour foreign to the first. The sitters were always sure that the controls were extraneous personalities, but the medium herself was never convinced, feeling there was another explanation. Later, when she had gained confidence and was less afraid of strangers, she lost the feeling that she needed this kind of protection, and began to carry on the same type of work in ordinary consciousness, and without any kind of guide entering into the process. To everyone's astonishment, including her own, the work did not suffer in any way, but, in general, continued to improve, though it was possibly not so spectacular or interesting to some people. Years later, after undergoing psychological analysis, she discovered the origin of her guides. They emerged during the analysis as representing different aspects of herself, which having had no outlet in life had become personalised. Had she been a novelist rather than a psychic, these guides would probably have led very satisfactory lives in one of her novels. It has been said that psychological analysis is likely to destroy any unusual psychic talent, whether perceptive or creative. This may be so where the analysis is of the purely reductive or destructive order, but where it is conducted with due recognition of the spiritual fabric of man, it can only be beneficial. In this case, it helped very much to clarify and focus the psychic perceptivity, by separating psychological material, which was subjective, from perception of objects which existed in the psychic field but were quite outside and independent of the percipient's mind.

Here is another case of a rather unusual nature. A woman with some mediumistic capacity was very ill. In order to cheer herself, she tried to do some automatic writing. This she was unable to do; but, while she was attempting it, she suddenly began to hear voices. These voices were those of a number of personalities, which became quite clear and definite to her. There was, for instance, Joan, who was a sentimentalist; Mary, a commonsense woman; Barbara, a nun; and there were two Pauls. Good Paul was a highly spiritual person, but bad Paul was a rake with a Rabelaisian mind, who behaved very badly. For instance, he would come into the bathroom when she was in the bath, and generally indulge in outrageous conduct.

The interesting feature, however, was that each and every one of these personalities insisted that he or she was not an outside entity but was showing her a side of her own character. She came for psychological treatment because she could never get rid of the voices and never had any peace. She knew that this was a dangerous state, and felt she must do something about it; on the other hand, she realised the value of learning so much about herself. It had been suggested to her that the entities were her guides, but she felt that this was not true. A striking thing about all this was that when these personalities were said, by outsiders, to be her guides, the guide-voices themselves showed their superior wisdom by disclaiming the position of being independent spirits. They were, in short, dramatisations of parts of her own mind.

In course of treatment the troublesome voices began to fade away, and the patient suddenly realised that Good and Bad Paul were one and the same person, Bad Paul being merely Good Paul trying to shake her out of her pruderies and prejudices. Incidentally, as the 'guides' became integrated with, and part of, her normal personality, she found that she was much better able to cope with her daily life, which was beset with a number of serious problems. A person of less innate understanding might well have felt herself to be either troubled by spirits, or else to be an important focus for a group of teachers on the other side. To the psychologist Paul was obviously the psychological archetype, known as the *animus*.

Again the guide—even if he be only a projection of the medium's mind—can serve yet another function. For, just as the aura of the circle may be said to go half-way towards making contact with the dead, while they themselves have to do the other half of the work, it may very well be that the guide is the channel through which the medium can really make a link with a dead person, which he could not make otherwise. For the guide, as we have said, represents that aspect of the medium which has dropped many of the limitations of the physical consciousness, such as shyness, fear of criticism, etc. But one of the most severe limitations to psychic perceptivity is the constant battery of the physical world through highly responsive senses. To pick up a telepathic message under conditions of full physical consciousness is like trying to hear a whisper in a boiler-shop. But the guide, while in control of the medium's body, rarely seems to be fully sheathed in it, but rather sits lightly, keeping such contact as enables him to use the breathing and organs of speech and hearing, and little else. Moreover, he seems to concentrate into himself the greater part of the powers of psychic perceptivity of the medium. Hence, it may be that the guide makes a contact with and can convey genuine messages from dead people in a way which would not be possible without him.

A guide may thus be any of the following:

1. A projection of the medium's own personality: which may be

(*a*) a dissociated 'complex' which may or may not include the power of psychic perceptivity,

(*b*) a personalised and dramatised symbol of the medium's wiser and deeper Self (i.e., an 'archetypal figure').

2. A dead person who is actually helping and controlling the medium in precisely the way he purports to be.

3. A combination of the above, the dead 'guide' playing telepathically into the medium's mind and not actually stepping into and controlling his body.

The only thing which is certain is that the guide is by no means always what he purports to be—i.e., a dead and wise person. In fact the weight of evidence goes to suggest that this is the rarest, not the commonest, of the possibilities.

The points raised above lead us on to the matter of what one may call the third phase in a séance. First the medium 'steps out' or, in scientific terms, dissociates. Secondly, another personality, or another aspect of the medium's personality, the guide, steps in and takes charge. This guide is endowed with whatever psychic perceptivity the medium innately possesses and the further psychic energy within the séance room enhances his powers.

In the third phase one of two things may happen. The guide himself may convey information or messages to those present, picking it, so to speak, out of the atmosphere. Or, yet another personality, or 'secondary control', may replace the guide, and speak directly through the medium. There may, of course, be more than one of these controls, and it often happens that a whole series of them manifest during one sitting, each one purporting to be a dead relative of somebody in the circle, or the guide of one of them. Yet another, but much rarer manifestation, is where genuine physical phenomena, such as any form of materialisation, take place.

These various things, different as they seem, are nevertheless related. For the information given, as well as the nature of the secondary control or, where physical phenomena occur, the pattern of the work can all be attributed to the type of the mentality of the medium. For instance, a Welsh peasant who is a physical medium will demonstrate a certain pattern of physical phenomena. This set pattern will tend to repeat itself, no matter whether his audience be of simple people like himself, or intellectual investigators. In short, it is personal to the medium himself, and only rarely adapts itself to the intellectual standard of the audience. Its tendency is to be always the same demonstration, but its ease and slickness vary considerably, according to the ease of the rapport of the medium with his group. Hence the next step is to consider what exactly is to be found in that psychic environment in which the medium works, and how and why any items in it should be selected for transmission through the medium to the sitters.

9

COMMUNICATIONS

To understand the source of communications coming from mediums, we need to go back once more to the question of the group aura, whether the group consist of two people, a whole circle or a large audience. In Chapter 7 it was described as including both the conscious and unconscious minds of those present, perhaps with something added.

This is true, but incomplete: because the exact nature of the aura thus formed is conditioned by, and becomes an instrument adapted to, the purpose for which it has been created. The aim of the circle is to get in touch with the unseen, and such is the creative power of thought that this avowed purpose becomes implemented by the mind, which fashions for itself a piece of apparatus to serve it.

In effect, that aura is at once an aid to the receptivity of the medium, much as a microphone will help one to hear sounds not ordinarily audible, or a cupped hand held to the ear is a help to the deaf, and an instrument which acts as a sounding board so as to amplify the vibrations which strike it. A taut piano string will vibrate and give out a true note when struck: but unless it is attached to a sounding board that note is faint and thin. It needs the board to make it powerful. A good instrument responds not only to the vibration of its strings; it reacts also to any note within its compass, from whatsoever source it comes. This compass, of course, varies. A glass tumbler or bowl echoes only the note which it will itself sound when struck, while the sounding board of a piano covers a range of several octaves.

So it is with a group. One group may have a very limited scope, corresponding to the minds of its creators, so that anything taking place in it will tend to repeat itself on the same small pattern, over and over again. Another may have a much greater variety of material of much better quality coming into it. This was noticed again and again by one of the writers when engaged in taking charge of circles, day after day, week after week, throughout a number of years. These shades and degrees are not, of course, noticed by the casual visitor, and seldom or ever by the person who sits in a circle infrequently, say once or twice a week. But when one's work calls for constant attendance, then by its very monotony it begins to pall, and one's attention becomes drawn to other things. Insensibly one's ideas clarify, and these rather subtle differences become patent.

Naturally, as we have suggested, the subjective contents of the minds of the sitters are a most important source of reaction in the group aura, for the simple reason that those very minds have created it. But any individual, including the medium, who is obsessed with some particular fad, will tend to bias the communications coming to the circle. Thus one well-known medium, for a whole year, insisted that most of his sitters had kidney trouble and should drink a decoction of dandelion leaves. The ideas coming from within the minds of those in the circle are, so to speak, the strings belonging to the instrument itself. Moreover, where the members of the group are self-interested and their thoughts and feelings cluster round themselves, they work in closed circles, and so the group aura will tend to be closed to impacts from outside it. But where the sitters have wide interests and are open to other ideas than those which concern themselves, the group aura is naturally more easily influenced by things from outside which, playing on the sensitive auric film, strike up a response in that film.

This principle is very important when we come to consider the various sources of the material brought into the circle by the medium or his guides, and we can classify it under various headings, according to its source. These are as follows:

1. *Subjective origin:* the minds of the sitters.
2. *Objective origin*:

   (*a*) Genuine communications from the dead.

   (*b*) Communications from other individuals, who are not dead.

   (*c*) Interpretations of thought-currents in the general collective. These may be either in the nature of personal statements, or else dramatised as if being made by an individual person.

   (*d*) Phenomena produced by non-human entities.

These divisions are arbitrary and theoretical: arbitrary because in practice the communications are often a mixture of things, and theoretical because of the very great difficulty there must necessarily be in sorting them out and putting them into their right pigeon-holes. We can, however, usefully discuss the various kinds of impulse which bring about the phenomena.

First, the subjective. This word is used because here the stimulus comes from inside the group. It is brought about by the thoughts and feelings of the members, and of nothing outside the circle. The factor which is likely to shut the circle up within itself is where, as we have said before, its members are really self-centred. Only too often a bereaved person shuts himself up with his grief as in a cocoon, and though he may think that he is sad and unhappy for the person who has died, he is really only grieving for himself. In any case, can there be genuine grief for people who have had the good fortune to be relieved of a sick or worn out body? We miss them terribly as a physical presence, where we have to endure a personal sacrifice; but if we think of them rather than ourselves, commonsense tells us they have won release, and that we should rejoice for them. It is entirely natural that we should feel hurt and in pain when a loved one dies, but persistent and exaggerated grief cannot be genuine without a good deal of self-interest creeping into it. In this way, the thoughts and longings about the dead person are, in fact, not directed at him, but at oneself, and they run in a closed circle, with oneself at the centre. Thus, given a whole group of people, each of whom is primarily thinking about himself, the general trend of the group aura will be to reflect that quality of inward-turnedness and to shut out whatever does not belong to this pattern. The inevitable result must be, however much one dislikes the idea, that any communications received are more likely to emanate from the vivid desires of the sitters' own minds than to come directly from the departed person. The case given earlier of the man and his daughter is here very much to the point. He frustrated his search by his over-concern.

It is not, however, conscious desires or thoughts alone which play an important part. These carry weight in giving the circle its special quality, but, as we have already said, the medium is much more likely to become the mouthpiece for ideas and memories, which lie in the less conscious part of the sitter's mind. When we remember that everything which anybody has ever known or seen makes a mark on the mind, it is clear that that mind will contain pictures of the person who has died, as well as a wealth of memories and events, mannerisms, tricks of speech, and all kinds of associations with him. The pre-occupation of the sitter with his loss will tend to bring these into prominence, even though he may carefully shut them from his conscious thoughts. A sitter has often been heard to say 'I carefully kept out every thought of my husband when I went to the séance!' What she overlooked was that the knowledge was in her unconscious mind wherever she might be. Hence, a medium can give a perfectly accurate picture of the person with whom the sitter wants to make contact, and purports to transmit a message from that person. He is probably sure that the dead person is present and wishes to communicate, but this does not by any means prove that he is in any kind of direct contact with him. What it does mean is that probably the medium has made a telepathic rapport with the thought-image in the mind of the sitter, and has identified himself with it. This identification is so strong that his power of dramatisation then enables him to take on the role of the dead person, and to give a convincing impersonation of him.

To sort out this very difficult question requires much observation and study of both mediums and sitters. For

Communications

mediums, to begin with, seldom if ever have any idea of what such a thought form is, and what it can do, nor do they recognise the difference between a thought form and the actual presence of a dead person. This is illustrated by the following experience:

A woman went to a séance, and was given by the medium a great deal of information about two people. They were both men. Their names and chief characteristics were given correctly. Then followed a lot of varied instruction from them, in their different roles. The medium spoke of their history, etc. The sitter asked if they were people on the other side.

'Oh yes,' said the medium, 'they have been out of the body some time, and are very anxious to get into touch with you.'

The truth was that one of the men was the sitter's neighbour at a dinner party the previous evening. He was, of course, still in the body, and the gist of his messages were an epitome of the conversation they had had together. The other 'communicator' was the hero of the sitter's new novel, which was not yet written, but which she had been pondering about for some weeks.

A further point needs to be stressed. Thoughts held in the mind of any person are not static, like a collection of photographs or waxworks. They come and go, form and dissolve, and seem to have a life of their own. This life is actually derived from the movements of the mind, conscious or unconscious, which generates them. Here is a story of a thought-form which, if it had caught the ordinary medium's attention in a séance, would almost certainly have led to his saying that a spirit was present and wished to give a message. This message, moreover, might very well have been about the fur coat in question.

Communications

Several of us were sitting in a friend's drawing-room over Sunday afternoon tea. I sat silent while our hostess and my husband were talking, when my attention was caught by a vague psychic formation beginning to develop behind her. This interested me because it seemed to have no association with anyone or anything in particular. But as I watched its growth, in the course of a few minutes it became more definite and finally shaped itself into the clear-cut outline of a sallow-faced woman with very dark hair, severely parted in the middle, and twisted into a graceful knot at the back of her head. She was very *soignée* and well dressed. The duck's egg green of her frock, and its design were extraordinarily clear. An outstanding feature was that round her neck hung a lovely row of large cornelian beads of a rich and vivid colour. They reached nearly to her waist. The figure showed no animation, nor did it seem interested in the talk, and so it puzzled me further. Looking at the form more closely, I realised it was a well-made thought-form. I was curious to see why it had been created. Breaking in on the conversation, I asked the hostess if she could identify the figure, which I described in exact detail.

'O yes! That is my friend P., who is now out in India.'

'Have you been thinking about her?'

'Yes, a great deal.'

'Were you thinking about her just now?'

'No! I was deeply interested in the conversation.'

'Are the beads right?' I asked.

At this she smiled, and said, 'They were the last gift she made me before she went abroad, and they are now upstairs in my jewel case.'

Then she added that the friend had written, not in any way referring to the beads, but asking her to sell her fur

129

coat. This had not been easy, and she had received only one offer, about which she had cabled to India, and which had been refused. In the last few days she had been wondering how she could do better for her friend.

This is a case, quite obviously, where the unconscious mind of the hostess was responsible for producing a life-like thought form, and with which it had associated the gift of beads. It is difficult to say why they had been brought into the immediate problem relating to the fur coat: nevertheless, they were a detail in a train of association. It may be that gratitude for the gift played some small part in energising the hostess to take a lot of trouble over the sale of the coat. It is a perfect example of the kind of thing which might influence a medium. And, as is well-known, it not infrequently happens that messages from people actually alive and well are delivered as if coming from the dead.

But it is not only real people who can thus appear and communicate. We have already been told of the fictitious fiancée who addressed the sitter in terms of endearment. The form was deliberately built up as an experiment, but the familiar endearments were added to it by association. At other times this sort of happening is not deliberate, but it happens all the same. A common instance of the development of such a thought-form may be found where a parent has lost a young child. If she goes persistently to séances, she may get apparent communications from the child. And year by year, as the child seems to grow older the quality of the communications changes, proportionately with the age which it would have reached. It is, however, most improbable that a child living in the psychic world, where, as we know, time is so plastic and fast-flowing, is going to hang fire and tend to develop—

assuming that it would develop under such circumstances —at the slow pace its body would require. It is far more probable, however, that the parent, holding in her mind that 'Eileen would be twelve, now', conditions the whole of the communications received in order to satisfy her more or less unconscious wish.

It is evident from such examples that a whole séance may take place successfully without the slightest shadow of a dead person coming into the circle: a fact which is disconcerting, no doubt, to some, but one which trained clairvoyance has, nevertheless, many times observed. Messages and communications have come through and have been honestly given by the medium. In fact, all that has taken place has been a more or less brilliant and quite unconscious display of mind-reading.

Under the second heading of our classification we come to the question of communication coming from outside the group. First, there are those genuinely from dead people.

We have, in the circle itself, an instrument suitable for telepathic rapport, the medium being the focus for its reception. It seems pretty certain that telepathy between people in the flesh does not take place at the physical level. No physical instrument has hitherto been able to detect any radiation between brain and brain which might represent thought transmission. But, what is more convincing, telepathy does not seem to answer to the mathematical laws governing any radiation in the physical world, such as the inverse square law, nor to take appreciable time to traverse great distances.

If, then, telepathy is a phenomenon of the psychic as distinct from the physical world; and if, as we have suggested, the dead, divested of their bodies, pass at once into the psychic realm and live there, functioning in their minds very much as they did in the body, there seems to be no theoretical reason why telepathy should not take place between dead and living people just as it does between people in the flesh. Hence, logic is on the side of genuine communication being possible, if the fundamental premises on survival are correct.

It is also logical to suppose that the dead themselves, if they retain their mental attributes, may wish to remain in contact with people they have left. A person naturally enough sends a telegram to his relatives to announce his safe arrival after a hazardous journey. Death, to most people, is such a journey, moreover, one from which there is no return—at any rate to the original home and relationships. Further, people who have been interested in certain subjects may find that they know somewhat more about them when released from the body (this is, of course, not to suggest omniscience, but that a wider consciousness may enlarge one's vision of the subject); and they may wish to try and pass some of that technical information to those with whom they were working.

Then, we may assume that there is not only the possibility, but perhaps also the desire of dead people to find channels of communication. Their main difficulty indeed may be that the people left behind do not know how to supply such a channel. They expect any communication to come in a certain guise and no other, or they close themselves in behind their feelings, or their minds are so busy with material things or with their own ideas, that the people on the other side can no more penetrate them than one can push a stick into a whirling flywheel. Sometimes, no doubt, there is an unexpected opportunity of putting a message through. The case of Margery may be cited as one, while the following two stories might have similar explanations.

Communications

'I was busy in the room where my husband was writing an article connected with psychical research. I suddenly became aware that there was a third person present. Looking at the visitor closely, I realised that he was neither a person physically alive to-day, nor had he the ordinary appearance of a dead person. He was like a person on a television screen, if one can imagine him in natural colours. This I gathered from the quality, texture, and density of the form. These details of assessment are extremely difficult to describe, because we have no language into which they exactly fit, but any good clairvoyant will know what is meant.

'This man was not tall, but thick-set and broad in the shoulders. He was dressed in a dark grey suit of old-fashioned cut. He had a heavy gold watch chain across his rather convex waistcoat, on which hung a gold seal, shield-shaped, and set with either dark blue enamel or a dark blue stone. On the shield was engraved the words "*Semper Fidelis*", and it had either some initials or a mark which I could not decipher.

'He was standing behind my husband, looking over his shoulder with shrewd and kindly amusement, as if reading what he was writing, though he was obviously *en rapport* with his mind rather than with any written word. He appeared to be keenly interested, and nodded approval several times in a perfectly natural way. He conveyed a sense of geniality and encouragement. It was almost as though he were saying, "That is right, get on with the job!", though there was not the faintest indication of any words or even message. It was much too implicit for that. After a short time he faded out, and I did not see any particular reason for his visit.

'Later in the day I fell asleep while resting, and dreamed

that I was talking animatedly to a famous psychical researcher, whom I had met in life, and who had died some eight or ten years before. We were discussing the question of life after death and the advances in modern research, when he broke off and said, "Now get on and finish that book. It is necessary to get the idea to the public. We must advance in these matters. You see, when we leave physical life we cannot remember words and certainly not things we have written. We remember our identity and ideas, but it is not at all probable we shall be able to establish exact data from this side, so do get on with the job!" I woke with a terrific jerk, just as though I had been catapulted back into my body. A thing most unusual to me.'

This vision and the ensuing dream can have one of two meanings. They might be nothing more than the ordinary psychological wish-fulfilment. The other meaning could reasonably imply a telepathic rapport between the writer, his wife and the small group of men who were pioneers in psychical research. It is purely a matter of personal choice which interpretation one may accept. There is neither proof nor disproof on either side, and it shows the dilemma in which ordinary spiritualism constantly leaves us. Actually, either of the above incidents alone might be pure hallucination or dream, but the two coming together, especially as the man in the vision and the man in the dream had been collaborators in physical life, perhaps weights the probability in favour of the less usual verdict.

The second story is of interest because it suggests contact both with a person unconscious or asleep as a result of drugs and illness and again with that same person very shortly after his death.

'A friend, whom we will call S., a well-known psychical researcher, was gravely ill, in fact dying, a thing which he and his family well knew and accepted without undue distress. He died early on a Friday morning. About two o'clock on the preceding Thursday morning I was wakened suddenly but without any shock to see what looked like a tall pillar of light standing by the side of my bed. In the pillar was S., looking ill as I had last seen him a couple of days before, but he was a great deal more vital. He smiled and seemed to know that I saw him, and said quite clearly a sentence in Latin which puzzled me because I do not know Latin. He was, by the way, a first rate Latin scholar. He evidently caught my bewilderment because he smiled again and proceeded to translate it into English. A moment or two later the light faded out.

'Next day I told S.'s wife the story and later on, to my dismay, she repeated it to S. himself. He was delighted because in some way the incident was highly significant to him, though he could not be asked to explain why, being too ill.

'On the Saturday evening after his death, I had a dinner party, and in the few minutes before the guests arrived I sat down to rest. The room was in darkness except for a bright fire, and I was alone. Then a light seemed to burst through the wall on one side of the room. To my utter surprise in that light was S., this time in ordinary day clothes, looking fit and well. Without preamble he said in a rapid voice, "Will you tell C. (his wife) that there is a certain paper in my wallet. It is in an inner pocket in my coat" and then he described the coat. "It is an important paper, I did not tell her what to do with it, and she will not know." He then said exactly what she had to do with it. At that moment my husband returned with the guests he had been out to fetch. I told them what had happened. Next day S.'s wife said she had discovered that paper, and was wondering what she should do about it.

She was very much relieved to receive the message and it was highly significant to her.'

This incident may be interpreted as either showing that people who are asleep, unconscious or dead, can move about and travel in their psychic forms. Or it may be that both are instances of telepathy from S. himself. Again the first incident might have been from S., and the second a dramatised version of Mrs. S.'s unconscious mind answering the question of which she was consciously aware. However much we may wish to believe one thing or another about all such experiences, there is nothing to guide us in the matter but personal choice, or a personal sense of conviction. According to our bias we have to make such a choice. The only other alternative is purely negative, that is, to refuse to consider such matters at all.

In principle, if one could find a circle consisting of exactly the right people, communication with the dead would be far more likely to be undistorted and real than in other groups. These people would need to be highly self-aware, mentally and emotionally unbiased and detached. They would have to be well on the way to being supermen—and nobody has reached that state. Moreover, if they had, they would doubtless find that any kind of circle was a clumsy and cumbersome way of communicating, and that they were able to achieve all they needed without the intervention of medium.

We have already mentioned the question of people not dead appearing at séances and giving messages. Reference to the chapter on survival will explain the rationale of this. Inability to interpret correctly in these cases lies in the lack of discrimination on the part of the medium and his control. It does not occur often, but, as most people know, it does happen.

Communications

What is of more moment is when the medium picks up out of the atmosphere ideas and thoughts which are common to the collective mind. These generally take the form of more or less well defined statements on politics or world events. They may take a prophetic tone, and they are often falsified by wishful thinking, as was so noticeable where the last war was concerned. In most cases the danger was denied or minimised, with the result that the actual communications were proved to be utterly false.

In 1940, just about the time of the fall of France, a group of us were engaged in discussing the latest developments in psychical research. A young journalist was with us, who suddenly fell into a half-way state and began to tell us that he was having a vision in which hordes of Germans were walking down the Strand and the Embankment, while the Thames was alive with them. He described himself as seeing this from the roof of a high building just off Fleet Street. Ultimately, however, they would be driven out again and all would be well. He went on in this strain for some minutes then suddenly stopped, appeared to wake up and the conversation went on. As we know, subsequent history showed the vision to be entirely false. But, at the time, the whole country was agog with fear and expectancy of invasion, and both the British and the Germans were visualising the likelihood of these things happening. The mediumistic young man —himself a writer and with a decided dramatic instinct— had been influenced by the contents both of his own mind and the collective and, while he was in a half-way state, these contents took on the form of a visual hallucination, which had no relation to any physical happenings which either had taken or would take place.

Communications

It is interesting, at this point, to note that a true interpretation of the contents of the collective is possible, and hence, that events can be anticipated long before the collective movement comes into the open. C. G. Jung, for instance, foresaw in 1918 the rise of Nazi Germany.[1] It was not, of course, an explicit and detailed prophecy. But already, before the 1914 war had been, as far as outward signs were concerned, lost to Germany, he saw from the dreams of some of his German patients the stirrings of primitive and savage forces, the emergence of the Blond Beast of Nietzsche. It was still a deeply buried thing—which, as we know, only began to become coherent when it was canalised through the mediumship of Adolf Hitler. Hitler was indeed 'controlled', the 'guide' being in this case Hitler's own darker nature, which belonged to the realm of the Blond Beast. In this instance, as in many others, psychological understanding was able to do more than mediumship, in discovering the trends of future history.

Another phenomenon occurring under this heading is that when a public figure, or one which means much to those concerned in circles, dies, that same person promptly appears in many séances in different parts of the world at the same moment. Thus W. T. Stead, a most important and significant figure in spiritualism in its early days, apparently controlled a whole number of mediums, approximately at the same time, quite soon after the news of his death had been received. One or two of these incidents were striking, the rest of very little importance. It is thus reasonably safe to prophesy that, unless mediumship alters considerably in the next few years, there will be an outcrop of simultaneous controls by some of our national heroes within a short time of their demise.

[1] C. G. Jung, *Essays on Contemporary Events*.

Communications

Needless to say, it *may* be that dead people can develop multiple personalities; or that they can send thought forms of themselves wherever they like. But it seems improbable that people who have been concerned with world affairs would be interested in appearing before small groups of people sitting in circles in their private parlours. On the other hand, both sitters and medium would be likely to be influenced by the removal from the scene of some great statesman, and it is this, primarily, that might lead to his supposed appearance in the circle.

The last heading, that of influence by non-human entities, is a much more debatable one. If it takes place, it is probable that they play a part in physical phenomena of the poltergeist order. But do such entities in fact exist? By many psychic people they are accepted as naturally as birds and beasts. Also, they have been believed in in every country, and in every period of history. Science can say neither Yes nor No, because it has no positive evidence; but it cannot *disprove* their existence. It is only pseudo-science which will be foolish enough to deny their existence in the face of mass belief, whereas no less a philosopher than Kant has stressed the bias towards a positive view of a belief which very many people have held for a very long time. The literature of occultism abounds in stories and references to such creatures, as do every religious scripture.

We have said that the classification we have made was arbitrary. It is only useful for the sake of clarity. And it must be pointed out that in practice, circles probably get mixed results. All of these need to be analysed with great discrimination before being accepted. The chief difficulty lies in making that analysis, and by what standard one can make one's judgments, and so feel any certainty of mind. This point will be discussed in a later chapter.

10

HEALING AND HEALERS

Sooner or later every student of psychic matters meets
that aspect of them which is connected with healing
the sick. It is as rich a field now as it has been for
thousands of years, for both the genuine healer and the
fraud, for the serious worker and the quack. For, as we know
only too well, there are many cases which, for one reason
or another, can be helped neither by orthodox medicine
nor by psychotherapy. These people are, therefore, apt
to run to anything or anybody who promises aid with
sufficient assurance, or who suggests that this may come
through mysterious and occult channels. There are thus
spiritualistic circles which give 'absent treatment' as well
as treatment on the actual circle, people who are reputed
to 'have the gift of healing', whether they work in full
consciousness, in trance, or otherwise. There are also a
number of priests of the Christian Churches who, following
an ancient tradition, hold services for the purpose of
sacramental healing. And, according to all accounts, it
would appear that something does occasionally really
happen as a result of these things, and that miracles do
occur.

Healing and Healers

The obvious and trite answer at this point is to say that all the people who benefit from them are hysterics, and that the cure is brought about by pure suggestion. There is some truth in this, but it is not the whole truth. An inoperable cancer, an organic nervous disease, and many other things which medicine cannot touch are not hysterical conditions, and some of the victims refuse to give in and go on seeking everywhere for a miracle. Usually they fail to find it. A retort to the suggestion theory, moreover, is that if such cures are brought about simply by suggestion, how is it that the sufferers are not already well? For even the box of pills or the nasty tasting medicine, not to mention the elaborate apparatus used in medicine to-day, already contain a strong element of suggestion, so that any cures brought about by 'healers' cannot be airily dismissed without confessing to a bad failure of the medical profession in the first instance.

The serious investigator, naturally, will want to check any results claimed, in much the same way as he would check the results obtained by some new drug. He wants conclusive evidence that, let us say, proved cases of cancer have got well while under non-medical treatment, and at once he finds himself in difficulties. For if he hears, let us say, that Mrs. Johnson had a cancer of the breast and it was cured by Dr. Wu, the Chinese guide of Mrs. Jones of Balham, and starts to make enquiries, he will probably find that his evidence boils down to this: that Mrs. Johnson is a convinced spiritualist. She felt slight prickings in the breast on waking up one morning. No, she did not see a doctor because she knew that Dr. Wu, that evening, would cure her. How did she know it was cancer? Dr. Wu said so. Next day the prickings had stopped. If the investigator is lucky, he may find that Mrs. Johnson had seen her doctor, who confirmed that there was a slight thickening in the breast, but not of a type to warrant drastic action at once. He had not seen her since. Or, if he had, he finds the condition neither better nor worse than it was. No, there was no question of a proven malignancy, though, of course, any such case must be watched.

This is rather typical of a case which falls down on investigation. Doctors' reports, X-rays, and reliable data are usually lacking, and, when a genuine case of some physical illness is reported as cured, it is *usually* of a type which can at times get well spontaneously. For even cancers occasionally die out without treatment, and before any success can truly be claimed in such an illness a series of them—not one alone—is called for. Thus if, let us say, one case in ten thousand of cancer gets well without treatment, and yet one out of every five hundred cases attending a professed healer were to get well, this would show that the healer was doing something definite. But the single case proves nothing unless there is reliable medical evidence.

This is one of the chief difficulties in investigating these matters. Another is that few people with serious trouble entirely give up their own doctor while they have their healing treatments. Hence, the cure resulting is just as likely to be due to the doctor as to the healer.

Then, of course, we have to take account of the vast number of people suffering from functional disease which a little common sense will put right; or from troubles with a hysterical origin, where a direct suggestion that they are better will have a marked, if temporary, effect on the symptoms. And it must be admitted that a group of patients at a healing séance are, for the most part, of a highly suggestible type, whether they are physically ill or not. That is not to say that they are necessarily unintelligent. Very learned people sometimes swallow quite uncritically what a medium says about their dead. Others become so much enthralled by the mysterious utterances of one who claims to have been a doctor during his earthlife that the most fantastic things are accepted by them as truth.

Unfortunately, only too often is one faced with something of this kind: a young woman stated categorically that she had had a psychic operation performed on her by the spirit guide of a medium.

'What for?' asked the doctor.

'I had an abscess round my appendix. Red Sunset cured the abscess and took the appendix out.'

'Were you ill?'

'No, I was not very well, but had nothing serious.'

'What made you think anything was wrong with your appendix?'

'Red Sunset said so.'

'Have you any scar? Was there any discharge from the abscess?'

'No, but I felt the operation going on.'

'Did it hurt?'

'No.'

'Well, how do you know anything was wrong and that Red Sunset did anything at all?'

'He said so. And he must know.'

This story is not an invention. Moreover, it is characteristic. In short, more nonsense is probably talked about psychic or spiritual healing than about any other aspect of the whole subject. But does this mean that the whole thing can be entirely dismissed? No—if only because of the age-old and universal belief in quasi-magical methods

143

of healing. For, as with other matters, these old beliefs somewhere contain a kernel of truth.

At this point it may be argued that this kernel lies simply in the suggestibility of certain kinds of people, so that they can be cured of psychological—and even sometimes of real physical—ills by methods which give them faith and make them believe they are getting well. But the serious and patient investigator will find ultimately that there is more to it than just that. In fact, he is likely to discover that what appear to be miracles of healing *do* occur, but that the more real they are, the less they are publicised and advertised. The most genuine healer, like the most spiritual-minded psychic, tends to shun publicity, not to seek it. Conversely, the more clamour there is about wonderful results, the less likely is the enquirer to find anything really satisfactory to the critical mind.

Thus, personal experience shows that the *principle* of spiritual and psychic healing stands, however unconvincing some practitioners may make it appear.

Certain distinctions need to be made between various methods of work. Chief of these is that between spiritual and psychic healing.

SPIRITUAL HEALING

It is scarcely necessary to-day to emphasise the very great effect of the mind or soul on the body. What is much less clear to us is the role of the spirit of man in matters of health and disease. The spirit expresses and manifests itself in space-time for a purpose. That purpose is a mystery to us: it is a thing of which we may have an implicit intuition. To try and express it is to distort it. 'The Tao that can be expressed is not the eternal Tao, the name which can be expressed is not the unchanging name', says Lao Tze; Tao being another word for 'Spirit'.

How that purpose is to be achieved is to the human mind a puzzle, because pain, suffering, disease, and death may very well be positive factors on the path of spiritual development, not evils which our little minds think should be eliminated at once. Thus, it may be the spirit in a man which plunges him into disaster, and the flight from that disaster may be, in truth, a refusal to accept the ordeal which the spirit demands. For spirit is concerned less with immediate personal contentment than with the bliss which comes when remote ends are fulfilled, less with the temporary satisfaction of the material aspects of man than with ultimate ends.

'The wind bloweth where it listeth and thou hearest the voice thereof but knowest not whence it cometh nor whither it goeth'—'wind' being, of course, the English for the Greek, 'pneuma', which also means 'spirit'.

The healing processes of the spirit may not always commend themselves to the limited mind of man. They may lead to miraculous changes and conversions of body and mind. They may lead to illumination and intense joy, or they may lead into the Valley of the Shadow. They may, on the other hand, lead a sick person to seeing the commonsense of going to a doctor and asking his advice. They may lead to healthy physical life, but death too may be the healing action of the spirit.

Further, the agent of the spirit, the true spiritual healer in any given case, may not himself be at all spiritually inclined. He may be the person who, because he gets angry and swears at you, shocks you out of your rut, and starts you off towards a new attitude of life. He may be the careless car driver who runs you down, or the person who steals your money and deprives you of luxury. He is not by any means necessarily an idealist or a learned person, though such persons often serve the purpose of the spirit. Hence, no person more than another has any right to claim to be a spiritual healer. He may, on the other hand, by his over-anxiety to be helpful, even delay—for he cannot frustrate altogether—the action of the spiritual process on the time-personality of the one he wants to help.

This does not, of course, mean that people should sit and do nothing. For, obviously, the spiritual role of any man is to use whatever capacities he has and can develop for the benefit of his fellows. And there are some for whom the care of the sick is a natural line of work, whether they try and do this on the physical or the psychic levels. Whether or not they become 'spiritual healers' in that work depends upon the depth of their understanding of themselves and of their motives in taking up the work.

Miraculous cures, as we have said, occur, though those most likely to be real are those one hears least about. Moreover, the real miracle-worker is often a most unsatisfactory witness, not necessarily because he is woolly-minded, but because his interest lies in spiritual matters and not in planning out a watertight case for himself. It does not matter to him whether or not he can answer the questions of an investigator, provided he feels he is serving his God. Hence we are up against characteristic difficulties in the case of the genuine healer just as much as in that of the spurious one. Moreover, here, too, single cases are apt to be less impressive or certain than a series. One hears people say, 'I don't know what X does with his patients, but it is amazing how they seem to get well', and it appears true that, without doing anything exceptional or spectacular, X achieves something which colleagues possibly more brilliant in orthodox medicine or in psychic understanding fail to do. That virtue of his may, indeed, be called that of spiritual healing, and there is not much more that can be said about it.

It seems probable that this spiritual quality lies at the root of all deep therapy, especially where mental problems are involved. It is what Jung calls, taking the phrase from African sources, 'the mana quality'. He tells us that in psychotherapy it matters more what one *is* than what one *does*. The person who is spiritually integrated has this 'mana quality', and anybody who makes a reasonable rapport with him may find that the very fact of contact changes something in himself. It is as if something had passed from the therapist to him and given him a new outlook on life, and hence greater health. This is a well-known phenomenon where mental health is concerned. It is probably fundamental in physical disease too, though here it works in conjunction with other factors. These factors may be purely physical—medicines, manipulation and the rest—or else psychic, directed at physical healing. It is principally with these psychic methods that we need concern ourselves, and try and understand the right and wrong of them.

PSYCHIC HEALING

The first point which needs to be made clear is that there are two aspects to any case. One is diagnosis, the other is treatment. Only too often it is taken for granted that a person who can diagnose disease by clairvoyance or other psychic means can *ipso facto* treat and cure it. This is obviously illogical, and is not true at this level any more than at any other. Doctors can diagnose cancer or heart disease, but that does not give them the power to cure it. It is the same with psychic diagnosis which, no matter how accurate and useful, does not confer either omniscience or omnipotence on the person who can do it. On the other hand, a trained clairvoyant may be able to clear up a point on diagnosis which remains obscure after the most thorough orthodox investigation, and may give a clue to treatment. Thus, many a difficult case has been cleared up by spinal manipulation under competent hands where X-rays completely failed to show in the spinal column trouble which was quite evident to the trained psychic eye.

In most spiritualistic circles diagnosis and treatment are given by the one medium or in the same circle. And, in view of the fact that positive and startling results are sometimes achieved, it is pertinent to consider how and why they may be brought about, as well as the reason for their failures.

THE HEALING CIRCLE

A healing group consists either of a private circle of friends, or of people connected with some organisation interested in psychic work. There seem to be two main types of these groups, one led by a negative medium supposedly under the control of a departed doctor or medicine man, and the other conducted without external control by an experienced worker who remains positive and conscious.

Healing and Healers

The medium who is successful in this work usually possesses natural powers of magnetic healing—a subject to be considered later—together with the faculty of sensing the condition of the patient. If such mediums are of a very negative order they take on the physical symptoms of the patient whom they are seeking to heal, and unless they understand the method of dismissing these symptoms it is not uncommon for them to reproduce the physical disturbance in themselves. This happens through the identification of the healer with the patient, and can be counteracted by a positive attitude of detachment which mentally refuses to take on the diseased condition. The attitude needed is not very different from that of any good doctor or nurse.

Sometimes the medium has clairvoyant powers and is able to see what is wrong with the person. The success of the curative side of this work in any case probably depends chiefly on the power of suggestion, with some help from the increased physical vitality given to the patient by psychic agencies.

When the healer works under a control,[1] the guide is invariably said to be someone who has been interested in healing or medicine in the past, and his ability to give such help as lies within the compass of his knowledge depends on the strength of his hold upon his medium. It is worth noting that a proportion of these mediums have been nurses or in some way associated with medicine already. A very usual control of this type is the American-Indian medicine-man, who is a powerful transmitter of vital energy, and without doubt he is often able to give at least temporary relief. Controls of this type have a faculty for giving such treatments and revitalising depleted bodies.

[1] See Chapter VIII on the nature of guides.

Healing and Healers

There are many varieties of this work, some soundly based and others ill-founded and unsatisfactory. Discrimination is of course necessary in accepting any advice given. There is a considerable amount of uncritical testimony in spiritualistic circles that genuine help has been received by these means.

The other kind of healing group works more definitely on devotional lines. Here the co-operation of invisible helpers is invoked, and a strong religious element is present. The group uses some method between meditation and oral prayer, the members bringing forward names and details of cases which are in need of help. The aim is to generate sufficient force by prayer and aspiration to send out healing energy to the sufferers, while the 'friends on the other side' attached to the group are also said to assist from the inner worlds to the best of their power. These friends are usually said to be discarnate human beings of much the same type as the sitters, interested in healing work and able to use psychic forces at 'astral' and other levels of the psychic world.

THE MEDIUM-HEALERS

These are people who have perhaps worked with a circle, or they may have discovered or developed their powers alone. In any case, they have this much in common; they all believe themselves to be working under the guidance of some agency higher than themselves, whether this guide be of the stature of Christ, or merely a wiser human being 'on the other side'. They are usually entirely sincere and honest people, sometimes humble in themselves, at other times inflated with a sense of their own

Healing and Healers

importance. But the healing is said to be brought about by the higher intelligence, the medium himself being simply an agent or channel for the power which comes through. Occasionally, in this work, as a result of some supposedly miraculous cure, their name gets into the press. What happens then is that, snowball-wise, their reputation grows, and people come from all over the country hoping to be healed. At times this proves a very lucrative proposition, but the majority of these people work largely for charity or for nominal fees or donations.

The point we have to consider is, what do these people do? All that has been already said about guides and controls holds good. If it does nothing else, the sense of moral backing suffices to give the medium self-assurance, and that is a great thing in dealing with certain types of people. That, however, is not the whole answer, because this kind of healer often has a certain intuitive sense of the cause of the trouble and how to handle it, combined with a faculty for directing vital energy to the site of it. This last is a faculty which science does not recognise, but which is well-known to psychic people, and forms the subject of the next section of this chapter.

A visit to one such person, a woman in the Midlands, gave a characteristic setting. In a large room twenty or thirty patients were waiting their turn, while in one corner the healer was at work. One after another the sufferers were brought up to her and set on a chair. The healer would ask what the trouble was and then proceed to do what she felt herself guided to do. There were many cases of backache, lumbago, sciatica, or rheumatism. In each of these the process was practically identical. First, the medium would move the affected joints with her hands, firmly telling the patient to let her do so. The definite

151

command, combined with a certain persuasiveness, often broke down the fear of pain and thereby allowed the painful part to be moved much more freely than would otherwise be possible and, very often, that is half the cure for such cases. Then would come some rather sketchy 'magnetic' passes over the area, after which the patient was possibly told something of this kind: 'That will be better now. Let's see you walk. Come along, put that foot straight on the ground . . . No, you can do better than that!' —and they did. Cases of cataract, diseases of the spinal cord, tumours and swellings did not do so well. The treatment in these latter cases consisted of passes and straight affirmation that they would be looked after whether they were personally present or not.

A very notable thing was the type of person in the room. They were for the most part highly suggestible, some of them even obvious hysterics. Few of them were people of detached mind, or able to reply boldly in the face of the healer's assertions, that they did not feel any different after treatment. Moreover, they were obviously people who were more prepared to demand and to take from life than to give—as witnessed by the fact that thirty patients deposited only some ten shillings in the 'gift' plate at the door.

When we talked to her after her clinic was over, the healer was found to be a good, honest and sincere woman, working from a conviction that she was doing a useful piece of work. She had no particular knowledge of medicine, but felt that her guides would tell her all she need know both about diagnosis and treatment. She was wise enough, perhaps as a result of practical experience, to know that there were many cases which would not be likely to benefit from the treatment, and on analysis the reason was clear: that the only really organic cases which got better were (*a*) those for whom movement of the part helped—and this would have been more skilfully and effectively done by an osteopath or a physiotherapist, (*b*) those who were suggestible—where a specialist in medical psychology would have done as well or better. Some alleviation of symptoms might follow, as a result of the revitalising of the tissues by the healer in other cases, but no instance was mentioned in which radical cure of physical disease could be considered even reasonably likely.

MAGNETIC HEALING

One interesting phenomenon which took place during the healing session described above was the extraordinary fatigue which one or two onlookers felt as time wore on. One, in fact, became so much exhausted that she had to be helped from the room and taken to sit in the fresh air for a while. Realising what had happened, and knowing something about these things, she soon recovered and all was well. The orthodox will probably fall back on the catchwords of hysteria, group-suggestion and the like; and, of course, one must allow of the possible truth of such a verdict. But another theory is that the healer had unconsciously drawn vital energy from those around her and used it on her patients. The analogy in ordinary terms would be that the medium had acted as a conductor of electricity from the stronger battery which was the onlooker, passing it on to the patient, with the result that the battery had become discharged. When the contact was broken, the battery regained its energy and all was well again. The fault was, of course, that the onlooker—

who, had she been less interested in what was going on, would have realised what was happening to her—had been caught unawares, and had not protected herself by a mental determination not to let herself be drained in this way.

To understand this principle better, it is necessary to make a digression. Scientific physiology to-day knows that the animal body is, from one aspect, an electro-magnetic apparatus. Every nerve-impulse, every contraction of a muscle, every physiological or psychological change in the body is accompanied by electrical phenomena. In some cases the bodily change produces the electrical discharge, while in other cases—such as impulses going from the brain to the periphery—it seems as if the electrical impulse came first. The phrases 'nervous discharge' or 'nervous energy' are in common use, but it is difficult or impossible to pin down those who use it to an exact definition.

From completely different sources comes an idea which may ultimately prove the clue. That is the Indian conception of *Prāna*. This is said to be a form of energy which —without going into elaborate details—governs the life and health of the physical body. This energy can be drawn into the body from the atmosphere; it exists in fresh foods; and the more vital and healthy a person is, the more he is said to be charged with this prāna or vital energy, while a sick person tends to be depleted either generally or in the particular area affected.

This is a very sketchy outline of a subject which is actually very complex.[1] But it must suffice for the moment, and it is adequate to explain certain forms of healing. For when a group rapport is formed, the members of it are in sufficiently close contact for the vital energies

[1] See *Vital Magnetic Healing* by E. A. Gardner, published by the Theosophical Publishing House.

of any one of them to flow into that group aura. Thus a depleted person may receive from it more than he had before, just as if an empty battery is linked up with others fully charged, the empty one will draw energy from the others. This, in parenthesis, is one reason why sitters in circles often do become deeply fatigued: the medium uses up a vast quantity of the vital energy while in trance, and tends therefore to draw on the sitters for supplies.

Certain people, however, either consciously or unconsciously, have the power to direct this energy to others and, by so doing, help to replenish them, to set stagnant and congested places going again, bringing about genuine results. Thus a pain may be relieved, either temporarily or permanently, inflammation may be reduced, 'nervous tension' with its attendant evils of insomnia, fear, or subjective pain can be relaxed, and so on. But solid objects like tumours or collections of pus are not usually moved, nor can broken bones be healed miraculously, even though the activity of the repairing cells may be considerably accelerated.

The phrase 'magnetic healing' is used for practitioners of this art because there is no other and more scientific phrase, and because they usually use their hands to make passes and sweeping movements over the patient, much as one would use a magnet to magnetise another piece of metal or a needle. It may also be an echo of Mesmer's conception of 'animal magnetism', which approaches roughly to the Indian doctrine of prāna.

The wise healer using this method neither gives his own vitality to the patient, nor does he draw on others around him. He relies on his ability to draw vitality from the atmosphere about him and acts as an impersonal channel for it. In any case there can be little doubt that it is the conscious or unconscious power of directing vital energy—quite apart from the direct suggestions made— to the patient which accounts for a great deal of the success of psychic healers.

Thus we have really three aspects of healing in this field: *spiritual healing*, which, as described, is not the prerogative of any one person or group, but which is a rare and precious quality quite unrelated to psychism or psychic practices. Then we have *psychic healing*, which is partly due to psychic or intuitive sense of what is wrong with the patient and what to do about it. This often combines with itself a certain degree of *magnetic healing* power. The latter, however, can also be found quite apart from any pretensions at psychic receptivity or at being guided or controlled from the inner worlds.

11

AIDS AND APPARATUS. SUPERSTITIONS

Prophecy, fortune-telling, and all kinds of divination are very ancient practices. They are known as the lesser occult arts and have fallen into some measure of disrepute among the intellectual *élite*, but they are still carried on in all classes of society and in many different ways. The common principle behind them, however, has never been discussed and, indeed, until the scientific establishment of the psi function, it could not be critically examined from such a basis. Some people work without any outside help, while many make use of some form of apparatus to help them to focus their powers, and so make it easier to formulate their findings. Tea-leaves, crystals, divining rods and many other things are used for that purpose. But whatever form, simple or complex, arbitrary and personal, or based on some general scheme such as one finds in cartomancy, the basis is the same; and that is the stimulation of the psi function in the mind of the operator.

The sceptic, of course, is inclined to scoff and to dismiss these practices as mere superstitions despite the universal belief in them. But there can be no denying that by means of them things are sometimes found out or foretold more

often than mere chance would allow. For if the mathematical odds against a thing being correctly prophesied
were, let us say, ten million to one, and yet out of every
thousand prophecies one were to come true, it is clear
that some factor other than chance must be at work. If,
for example, a person is told by somebody using cards
that he will take a journey across water, then the odds
are probably considerably in favour of his taking that
journey, say, by crossing a bridge over a stream, and the
prophetic element can be discounted. But if the same
person, having no intention of going abroad, is then told
in the next breath that something quite unusual is going
to take place and it does, then the honours go to the
fortune-teller.

This actually happened in an instance where a card-
reader said, 'I don't understand this. It looks like an
aircraft coming down and not going up again.' Then in
answer to a question she went on, 'No, it's not an accident.
But I can't tell you any more than that.' Within a fort-
night, the person about whom this was foretold made a
sudden journey abroad, and on the return booked his
passage by air from the Mediterranean to London. All
went well until he landed in Paris, when he was told,
'You can't go on as there is fog in London', and finished
his trip by rail and boat. Such a prophecy working out
in this way is unlikely to be a matter of chance, especially
as the trip took place in summer.

Still more striking is the account which follows. For
here we have, not one single instance of prophecy, but a
number of them, all of which came true.

'I (P.D.P.) was motoring in the Highlands with two
friends, when we unexpectedly came upon a gypsy encampment by the roadside. My hostess exclaimed, "The

158

gypsies have returned. Would you like to have your fortunes told?'' I refused at first, but suddenly altered my mind. We retraced our steps and, although at first sight the encampment seemed deserted, two gypsies appeared at once.

'The elder woman gave us a brief glance then took me and one of my friends into her caravan, while the younger took my hostess into her own tent. The swarthy, black-eyed woman asked me in the usual way to cross her palm with silver, then she lightly touched my finger-tips for a moment, shut her eyes and poured out a torrent of speech. Her character-reading was astonishing; and she mentioned without hesitation a number of incidents in my past life. She was particularly clever in her analysis of my psychic abilities, seeing both their weakness and their strength.

'Eventually she began to foretell the future. It sounded incredible, not to say impossible. She sketched correctly the kind of professional life I was then living and said that it would change radically. "You will marry a man who is either a doctor, or who is in a profession associated with sharp, bright instruments'' she went on, adding various details about him. "You will work together and write books together. You will travel together and neither of you will work alone in the future.'' She then foretold a number of events which would lead up to this. Then, guessing my doubts, she said, "You don't believe me, so I am going to tell you three unimportant things which will come true within the next seven days. When they do, you'll remember what the gypsy said, and you'll see that in the next few years the big things will happen too.''

'She then told me that I should very shortly receive a gift of stones; that I would also be given a ring; and that, on some very stony ground, I should find two sprays of white heather where no other white heather grew.

'I said nothing of all this to my hostess, but that evening while I was dressing for dinner she came into my room, bringing a box of unset cairngorm stones, beautifully cut. She said, "I got these for you for last Christmas. But you will remember that I had 'flu and was too ill to send them off. So here they are." Three days later, a registered parcel arrived from London. It contained an old ring and a note from a friend who said, "I meant to leave you this ring in my will, but I don't see why you should not have it now, so I am sending it at once." Then, on the fifth day we were out for a picnic and on the way home, as we went through a very desolate pass in the hills, my hostess said, "There's rather a fine cairn just at the top of this hill. Let's climb up and have a look at it". I had nearly reached the top of the rough and stony track when I saw, growing in solitary beauty, two sprays of white heather. There was not another scrap in sight.

'I confess that I was impressed, when these odd events came true exactly as had been foretold. I was still more struck when the larger issues developed, especially as they represented a turning-point in my life such as I had never even contemplated.

'It is worth recording that when the gypsy's torrent of language had spent itself, she turned to my friend, but her half-crown was rewarded with nothing more than the usual fortune-teller's gibberish which one so often meets with at fairs or at the seaside. There was nothing in it but commonplace generalisations, while the bits of character reading were quite wide of the mark.

'The striking thing was that one of us was treated to real and startling precognition while the other was given nothing of value. In the first case the gypsy seemed to have tapped a live wire of information and could scarcely keep pace with what she saw, while in the second, it was as if one had put a coin into a machine and received a packet automatically and mechanically thrown out in return.'

Naturally, such definite instances are rare, but they occur quite frequently enough to show that there are times when something is working in the operator's mind which opens the future up to him, if only in an imperfect and patchy way. Much the same may be said of such things as dowsing for water or metals. The contention of some people that this is pure guess-work, or else due to an assessment of physical conditions, simply will not stand when many cases have been carefully studied. There is much careful evidence on this matter, which can bear close scrutiny.

The arts of palmistry and astrology come into a somewhat different category, because both of these are based on scientific or mathematical data. The hand, like the face or the general configuration of the body, can tell you a great deal about a person without your resorting to any further explanation, and indeed books have been written on the subject which are fully up to the standard of any medical text-book. But we have to consider also the extraordinary things sometimes told by uneducated people like gypsies to whom any scientific study is completely strange. The same may be said to apply to graphology and numerology.

Astrology is worked out on a basis of pure mathematics in connection with the position of the planets and stars at the time of birth. Here we are faced either with the fact that the extraordinarily accurate readings of astrological maps without the astrologer ever having seen the person are purely psychic or intuitive, or else with a mystery which goes deep into the question of the relationship of man with the seemingly objective world, whether as shown in the heavens or in the more mundane sphere of everyday contacts. The fact, nevertheless, remains that even orthodox psychologists, some with a prejudice against such seemingly fantastic notions, have found themselves forced to realise that an expert astrologer can be of very real value in assessing the type and capabilities of a person whose horoscope he has made. He can for instance predict such things as whether two people are likely to find marriage easy or difficult, creative or frustrating, whether there is a critical phase of life pending, and how the person concerned can best deal with it.

There is also another aspect of these things on which groups of workers are trying with more or less success to work out a scientific basis, and this concerns the diagnosis and treatment of disease. Some of the best work in this direction has been done with a simple divining rod made out of two pieces of flexible whalebone. Others use pendulums, while yet another group devises elaborate electrical apparatus which is only too often connected up in defiance of any known laws of electricity—and which, incidentally, works just as well when it is not connected up at all, *provided the operator does not know this*.

The reader may ask at this point why we have lumped such many and diverse things into one chapter without explaining any of them in detail. The fact is that there is a common denominator to all of them, whether or not they have any objective scientific basis. It is this aspect of them only which is relevant to this book. A more detailed study can be made from any of the mass of books on the

Aids and Apparatus. Superstitions

various subjects mentioned. For it is the psychic perceptivity of the operator which, in every case, is the clue to the results. In fact we may go further and say that it is probably this which makes for the best results in any sphere where human relationships are concerned. No matter how well and accurately a doctor may use his instruments, how well trained a teacher may be, there is always something more about the one whose work is of the finest quality, something that does not depend upon his intellectual abilities but goes beyond them. This extra factor is in effect precisely that which the gypsy uses when she is right in her predictions or character readings, and is the extra-sense which we call intuition, psi, paracognition, or psychism, according to our vocabulary.

The value of any kind of apparatus, whether it be cards, sand, a rod, a pendulum, electrical apparatus, or more orthodox and scientific means of getting data about a person, is that it can act as a lens to focus the psychic perceptions, or as a screen on which the image can be thrown and so made visible.

If we take tea-leaves, sand, or the bundles of sticks which are used in China and thrown on the ground, there can obviously be no set pattern which can be read as a book is read. Here, as where a crystal is used, the reading depends on a slight degree of self-hypnosis in the operator, which allows images to form in his mind. If we use an ink-blot such as psychologists make for the purposes of the Rorschach test; or, for that matter, if we look at the patterns made by cracks on the ceiling or irregularities in the paint on a wall, we find ourselves seeing shapes in them, and say that they look like this or that thing or person. It is only going a step further for these pictures to become animated and perhaps to acquire something of a dream-like quality. Usually they are derived from associations in our own minds and have only a personal significance. But the fortune-teller seems to have placed himself in some measure of telepathic rapport with the person who is consulting him, and if he can eliminate his own associations from the pictures he sees, they may be found to relate to the client and not to the operator. Without them he would usually be unable to focus what his telepathic rapport tells him, and to express it in any useful terms.

Fortune-telling by cards is somewhat different in that the usual method is for the client to cut and select them from a pack provided. These are then spread out on the table and the reading given. Here the mind of the client is part of the operation, in that he chooses at random where he will cut the pack and what cards he will pick out. But the random element seems to be unconsciously directed by purpose, so that the cards which are picked out provide a basis for the reader. What then follows, if it is to be of any real use, is usually something more than can be found in the books which tell you what each card means. It is, in short, the individual interpretation which counts more than the rule-of-thumb reading, which only too often means little or nothing. Of course, the question of telepathy must also come into the picture; and the same principle applies to phrenology, palmistry, and the lesser occult arts in general, and serves to explain why it is that so often a pseudo-science gives results which, by ordinary rules, it should not give.

When we come to analyse water-divining, we have a rather strange phenomenon, in that the rod used seems to move on its own volition when the diviner crosses the underground stream of water. The same is said about the pendulum used either for that purpose or for diagnosing and prescribing for disease. But in no single case, as yet, has any apparatus been devised for such divination which does not directly or indirectly involve the human element. That is to say, in all of them the musculature of the human body is involved. Pendulums suspended on a gallows will not work unless a human finger is on the gallows, and hence capable of imparting minute impulses to it. A divining rod must be held in a peculiarly unstable grip; while the electrical boxes so far designed all involve the tactile or auditory factor of the operator, and do not record their findings simply on a mechanically operated dial or gauge.

What seems to happen here is that the psychic perceptivity of the worker operates through the unconscious mind, and causes the muscles of the arm or hand to move the rod, swing the pendulum, or otherwise indicate what is required.

Where direct psychometry, crystal-gazing, or geomancy are concerned, the data obtained psychically are translated through the conscious mind of the reader. With the rod or pendulum, on the other hand, it is as if the unconsciously received data short-circuited or by-passed the conscious mind and produced reflex nervous actions instead. That this is so seems to be shown when one of us (L.J.B.) tried to find water. He failed completely when he actively thought about water, but when he purposely distracted his mind from the subject and tried again, the rod he held suddenly and violently moved when he crossed the proper place. Similarly, in trying to locate with the rod a magnet placed on the edge of a table, he found that nothing happened automatically as he moved the rod along past the magnet. But it worked either when he took his mind off the subject entirely, or when, instead of this, he made mental images of the probable relation of rod to magnet, and deliberately dipped the rod when the images coincided. In the first experiment, he had to let the whole process take place unconsciously, whereas in the later part of the second, he was really indulging in a piece of minor clairvoyance, which made the rod quite unnecessary except as a pointer.

A further matter about all these things is the mental orientation of the operator. If, for instance, he believes that to diagnose disease his pendulum must be made of ivory and hang on silk, he will fail to get results if he ties the indiarubber on his desk to a piece of string. But his results will be just as good if he thinks that the latter will work. The same applies to the divining rod, where the traditional hazel-twig can be advantageously replaced by anything springy such as whalebone, clock-spring, or even stiff wire, provided the diviner will accept this as adequate. As regards the complicated apparatus used, it would not matter in the least if the inside were taken out, provided the operator either believed that it was there, or else accepted the fact that this inside was unnecessary. One bold doctor went so far as to use his apparatus merely as a convenient standard of measurement and assessment and for no other purpose, training himself to diagnose his patients chiefly out of his own thoughts about them. Thus, he would think about X and then try out with his machine whether there were, let us say, streptococcal infection present. If the result were positive, he would then think, 'Throat', 'Chest', 'Abdomen', and so on until he was satisfied he had located it. His results were surprisingly accurate, even though most of the time he did not bother to make what were supposed to be the proper connections of wires to the machine at all. Similarly, one expert and highly accurate operator of the divining rod for medical purposes realised that he could reverse the action of the rod at will. Thus, he could either make it dip when he wanted a 'Yes' answer, or he could make it dip at the moment when the reading would no longer be positive and he wanted to be told 'No'. This man, a skilled surgeon, was quite aware of the fact that his mental orientation was the factor which governed the action of the rod. If, for instance, he were seeking for a septic tooth, he would wish the rod to dip when he was over that tooth: a 'Yes' reaction. But if, for instance (and this is a hypothetical case: nevertheless, it avoids a long and irrelevant technical parenthesis) he wished to ascertain the size of an enlarged spleen, he might wish his rod to remain up so long as it was over the splenic area but to dip the moment its tip passed over the edge of it: that is, to give him a reaction in the negative. He might then check his result from this means of using the rod by coming at the spleen in the reverse direction. He would approach the spleen from outside, and now wish his rod to dip when it reached the edge of that organ: that is, to give him, a 'Yes' reaction. It was rarely that he was found to have made a mistake in any matter which could be further proved by X-ray or other ordinary means.

This is in no sense disparagement of the work of people who use these aids. On the other hand, there is no ground for the one who can wield a rod to feel superior to others. Some people work with tools, others without, and that is the whole difference. It is true that there is a tendency for the use of apparatus to be more spectacular, as well as more convenient than direct, unaided perception. It attracts the less critical and scientific minds and hence much nonsense is talked, but there are also a number of serious and scientifically trained people who use it. Nor is it a denial of the validity of such attempts as have been made at establishing wave-lengths for disease and trying to determine the kind of radiations which come from different metals. These things may be perfectly accurate, despite the fact that orthodox science does not know anything about them. We are concerned only with giving an explanation of some of the incongruities which careful examination of the phenomena show, and which do not accord with what is said about them and their supposed mode of action. The only conception which makes the many contradictions consistent is that of the unconscious action of psychic perceptivity through whatever outward aid or apparatus is used by any particular person.

A matter that cannot be left out of this chapter is that of superstitions. The kinship with fortune-telling lies in the precognition of something which is about to happen. But in the case of superstitions it is an automatic and spontaneous thing brought to light by some trick of behaviour or by the unconscious performance of a certain act traditionally said to be unlucky. For it is only too well-established in the minds of people that certain superstitions inevitably work. Naturally, one has to discount a great deal of this belief. Still, there are certain cases where the facts are beyond dispute. The question is, why? Is it possible that walking under a ladder or spilling the salt will produce an accident? The answer is, certainly not. But if one is unconsciously aware of some misfortune to come, one may very well find oneself walking under the ladder and thereby drawing attention to the fact that trouble is on the way. An independent observer might be able to tell us that we had walked under a ladder a dozen times in the last month *without* noticing that we had done so, and without any calamity befalling us.

One of us is in the habit of making regular written contributions to a certain organisation, and in two years none of these had been rejected. On the next occasion he commented aloud on this and immediately tried to cover himself by lightly remarking, 'Touch wood!' and doing so. Next day one of his articles arrived back with a request that it be emended: clearly the neutralising magic had not worked. He was not surprised, because as he made his remark he was suddenly aware that it had been caused by an underlying knowledge that all was not well and that, for some reason, his last paper had failed to please. Yet, as far as he knew, this particular article was up to standard and no different in any material way from a score of others which had been accepted. Maybe he was mistaken and the whole thing may have been coincidence. But it did not *feel* so to him.

It is not an uncommon thing either that certain events appear to be omens of a death in the house or family. In at least three instances of unrelated people, if any of them happened to see a white owl during daylight, it was followed by a death within the next year or so. Does this mean that some unknown god sends the owl across their path as a warning? The answer is probably much simpler than that. White owls are not often seen at any time, but they are not exceedingly rare. If, on the other hand, somebody has a precognition of the death of his mother, and there is established in the collective unconscious of his family or group some tradition that seeing a white owl heralds such an event, then he may unconsciously

169

have his attention drawn to the owl because of his pre-cognition, whereas at other times he would not have noticed it at all. Similarly, such a precognition may be the unconscious cause of a person breaking a mirror or walking under a ladder which he would not have done otherwise. In other words, one may say that if one consciously or unconsciously believes in a superstition, and if one dis-counts the many times one may, for instance, walk under a ladder without noticing one has done so, then it may prove effective in the direction it traditionally assumes.

One must, at the same time, realise that precognition is not by any means always at the root of these things. For if a person should, for one reason or another, be nervous and expect an accident, he may well be the direct cause of that accident taking place. Thus, one woman had, because of a number of mechanical break-downs in a particular car, lost her faith in that car. None of the difficulties were in any way such as would cause any greater calamity than being stranded at the roadside, and the car seemed mechanically sound as to brakes, steering, and all the things which might otherwise lead to danger. But her distrust might have caused her, or by telepathy, her husband, to become nervous, and without any conscious volition on either side, might have made whichever of them was driving do the wrong thing and have an accident. An unintelligent person would then say, 'I told you so. I knew psychically that this would happen', not realising that she was the cause of the trouble and that, if she had not been afraid, it would not have happened at all.

On the other side of the picture we have the couple who set out for a drive and, without either saying any-thing to the other, each was curiously nervous. At a later stage, while they were standing still by the roadside, a bus crashed into the back of their car without the slightest excuse for doing so and through no fault of their own. Each one, as they owned to one another afterwards, felt a feeling of relief when this had happened, because they knew that the anticipated trouble was over and the result not as bad as they feared it might be. Here, clearly, precognition was at work.

Thus, superstition may sometimes be a form of precognition of disaster or success, and is quite intelligible on rational grounds. But this does not mean that intelligent people are justified in giving way to every whim, or should believe in every old wives' tale about these things, because, the more positive and clear-sighted they are, the less they will need indirect methods of telling them what is going to happen, and the more their own awareness will enlighten them directly.

This analysis of the possible mechanism by which superstition may work is, we think, tenable. It undoubtedly serves to explain some instances, but our knowledge of the relationship between cause and effect in the psychic world is still very scanty and there are probably other and less simple answers to the problems which the subject raises. It is, for instance, unlikely that the banshee met with in connection with certain Irish families is covered by the explanations we have put forward. This, however, is outside the reach of our present objective knowledge. There are many mysteries still about psychic matters, and we are only on the very fringes of understanding the laws which operate them.

12

OBSESSION AND POSSESSION

Sooner or later, the student of psychic problems is sure to come up against the matter of obsession or possession by evil spirits. This is an age-long and universal belief, and on these grounds alone, the same weight must be accorded to it as to other traditions. But to attribute the majority of acute mental troubles to this cause is, to say the least of it, an exaggeration. In any case, a proper understanding of *how* such possession comes about—if it does—can only help to diminish the danger of it ever taking place at all, as well as allaying the very real fear which some people feel at the possibility.

If a person who is open both to the principles of psychology and to the existence of an objective psychic world looks at the subject, he will see two theoretical possibilities. One is that a malicious denizen of the psychic spheres, whether human or non-human, is the active agent which troubles an innocent victim. It does this in one of two ways: either it takes possession of him and makes him behave outrageously and insanely, or it obsesses him from outside, dinning obscene suggestions into his ears, telling him to commit this or that crime, showing him

172

Obsession and Possession

terrifying or disgusting visions which he is unable to shut out. This is the 'psychic' interpretation, one far too readily accepted by some people.

The other possibility is that possession or obsession is not due to any outside entity, but that it comes from within the mind of the victim and is therefore self-inflicted. That this is a thing which *really* happens is more than theory. It is a commonplace event, known to any experienced psychotherapist or psychiatrist. Does it entirely dethrone the traditional belief? The answer, as in other cases, is that it does not, but it supplies a principle which is complementary to the idea of possession by devils; and besides, it shows how, if this doctrine is true, troubles which result from it can be safely and surely prevented.

Let us begin by looking at each theory separately. Do spirits—i.e. independent psychic entities with a life of their own—exist? Tradition tells us that they do, and psychic experience confirms this. But it does not follow that such entities are in themselves evil: they only become so when they cross the path of man. Then, if they should interfere with human beings, they are, from his point of view, evil. A tiger in the jungle is no more wicked than a wild deer or a humming-bird: he lives according to the laws of his nature and it is right that he should do so. Put him in a village, however, and the result is havoc. The evil is not in the tiger but in his being in what, from the viewpoint of man, is a wrong environment. Some psychic entities can thus be classed as malignant, in the same way as others can be called benevolent, because they happen to fit into our scheme of things in a way which seems beneficent to ourselves.

The possession theory postulates that such an entity breaks into the house of the personality of the victim,

173

takes possession of his body much as the control is said
to take over the body of a medium, and proceeds to run
riot with it. Indeed, it is not always easy to say that this
is not so. How, for instance, account for the case of the
Arab boy who had never seen the sea, nor heard English
spoken, nor met an Englishman previous to encountering
the visitor who reported the story to us? This boy had a
kind of fit and while he was in it he spoke the colloquial
English of an uneducated man, saying things which suggested that he was possessed by a rough type of British
sailor. When the fit ended, the boy recovered and reverted
to his purely Arabic personality and speech, remembering
no word of English nor of what had transpired. Many
such stories are to be found, though few of them are any-
where near being evidential.

A somewhat different order of event is where, for instance, a series of suicides take place in a certain room.
There is usually no connection whatever between the
individual people who kill themselves, and they have no
inkling that it has ever happened there before, until the
place develops a reputation for being unlucky or haunted.
The easy explanation is that some evil spirit lives in the
room, takes possession of the victim and drives him to
the act. The idea of obsession rather than possession is
probably nearer the truth, at least in most cases: that is,
something in the room suggests suicide to the people who
sleep in it, until the idea becomes too strong for them,
and drives them over the edge. It may, of course, be that
the original suicide still haunts the place, earth-bound. It
is much more likely that there is no specific entity at all,
but rather a kind of psychic miasma, an atmosphere left
by the first person to kill himself there, enhanced by others
who subsequently succumbed to the same temptation.

Obsession and Possession

If the theory of psychic possession or obsession is accepted, there is an obvious remedy—also a traditional one: exorcise the entity, drive the usurper out, and all will be well. One finds many people who believe this idea and who try to treat the hysterical, the epileptic or the insane on these lines. The trouble is that it does not work. Any improvement which may take place is usually due either to the temporary power of suggestion or, perhaps would have taken place anyway in the natural course of events. Only in rare instances can any link be thought to exist between exorcism and a real cure; and this is more likely to be due to a form of 'conversion', or cure from within the individual than because a devil has been driven out of him.

Moreover, there is an aspect of the matter which is only too readily forgotten, which is that if a burglar breaks into a house and is then removed, this does not close the door or window through which he got in. On the contrary, unless the owner takes positive steps to mend matters the house remains wide open to all comers and a temptation to others to enter it.

The psychological explanation is also on the lines suggested in discussing the nature of mediumship and control. Certain people repress aspects of themselves which they think are unworthy or immoral. All goes well, or at least, appears to go well, until the repression breaks down, when their ordinary standards of behaviour go by the board, and it looks as if some entirely different being possessed them. A very common example of this is where a mild-looking person, provoked beyond endurance, goes berserk with fury. For the time being, he is completely out of hand and literally 'beside himself'. His ego has lost hold and has been dislocated, and he is carried by torrents of emotion which had hitherto been held in leash. But—

175

and the discerning eye may have anticipated such a development—this emotion is nothing new: it was in him the whole time, pushed under the surface by psychological inhibitions. It was dissociated from consciousness and thereby became explosive and dangerous. Anger, sex, panic fear, any of the cruder emotions, may be kept in such a state. It only requires a sufficient weakening of the surface consciousness for them to burst through and cause violent and hysterical scenes. Such a weakening may come from long attrition and frustration, from ill-health, abuse of alcohol or other drugs, shock, severe fatigue or starvation. It is to be noted that one of the prevalent causes for these outbreaks is 'sitting for development' or unwise automatic writing. The deliberate renunciation of conscious control of oneself is one of the most potent means of causing 'nervous breakdown' of this order.

The victim is indeed possessed of a devil: the devil created by himself and within himself as a result of repression. Usually, once the outburst is over, the person settles down and returns to normal, until once more, the internal pressure becomes great enough to blow the lid off and allow a further eruption. In other cases, once the dam is broken, it is broken irretrievably and the patient enters a new phase of life. It may be that the hitherto prim spinster becomes little more than a harlot, the weak 'yes-man' becomes aggressive and fights in and out of season. Or, if the process can be given a constructive turn, the energy which gave rise to the original outburst is led into creative channels and the individual begins to grow into a positive, integrated person. In other instances, the experience is permanently shattering and the ego is unable to take control again. This is insanity.

A state of affairs still more dangerous, in that it is apt

to drag others with it, occurs when the cause is not so much an invasion of repressed personal material into the conscious mind, as of the collective. This collective mind, is as one would expect, vastly more powerful than the single mind, and any irruption of it into the individual field is apt to cause serious and permanent damage. This is a simple statement. To go into it fully would require far more space than can be given to it here. Besides, it is a highly intricate and technical matter. This much can be said: that the victim is apt to feel himself to be the channel for tremendous forces and to identify himself with the gods, if not with God. In his own estimation, he is a superman. The disaster which takes place under such circumstances is one we have seen in the person of Adolf Hitler. Hitler in his own right, was an insignificant little man. He unconsciously developed mediumship: not in this case in order to make contact with the dead, but so as to express the deeper and more murky aspects of the collective German mind. As Jung pointed out already in 1937, he was great *as a medium*, and as his development became more and more successful, so did the personality of the little paperhanger atrophy, to be replaced by an ugly, monstrous creature embodying in personal form the evil he had elected to serve. All went well with this creature until it was thwarted, when deterioration set in and insanity overcame its agent.

In lesser degree, we find many people who, becoming inflated with powerful Messianic ideas, are in much the same state as Hitler. They are like clouds highly charged with electricity, 'possessed' by that charge, and unless they find some lightning conductor to diminish the tension, there may be a moment of sparking which will blast them out of the normal world for good.

Obsession and Possession

Such is the purely psychological explanation of the kind of disorder which some spiritualists and psychics tend to attribute to the attacks of evil spirits. It amounts to this: that the evil spirit is indeed there. But that it is self-generated and is a creation simply of the mind which falls a victim to it.

We have, however, said that in our opinion, dangerous psychic entities do indeed exist in their own right. *Neither of us has yet seen a single case whether among the sane or the insane whose condition could not be explained along the line of psychological principles.* This point is worth underlining, in view of the fear which the notion of psychic attack and invasion has for some. Maybe in the East, where people are much less firmly anchored to their bodies than they are in the West, things may be otherwise, but they are probably more so in degree than in principle.

This principle is probably one which embraces both the psychic's and the psychologist's points of view and is that the only hold which an evil entity can obtain on a human being is if that person has in himself something of the same quality as the entity itself. That is, the door is opened from *within* the psyche, otherwise nothing can enter. 'No harm can touch the pure in heart', but if, for instance, a dead drunkard should try and control a live body so as to go on indulging his craving for alcohol, he will not be able to do so unless the person to whom that body belongs has already, actively or latently, a weakness for drink or some other kind of drug.

This also explains the falsity of the general assumption in spiritualistic circles that to open a séance with hymn or prayer creates a protective atmosphere, in which unpleasant events cannot occur. They are often distressed to discover that this is not so in fact. The answer is that the negative material is in the sitters themselves, and that no external protective 'magic' can always hold this under, especially where people are practising relaxation in order to go into trance. The religious nature of the prayers may clear the general psychic atmosphere at the beginning, but it does not alter the minds of the medium or sitters. It is as if one ventilated a room and cleared the smoke out of it, then shut the windows only to find that the fire in the room itself was the cause of the trouble.

If an exorcist should expel a possessing entity, he leaves the person attacked in the same state of mind, unless definite steps are taken to change it: the heel of Achilles is still unprotected. The only way to a radical cure, if such be possible, is if the victim will realise the weakness in himself and do the work necessary to remedy it. This calls for self-analysis, leading to self-awareness, even of his darkest aspects. After that he needs to use his will in a resolve to mend his ways and break the old bad habits of thought and feeling.

The same may be said of the would-be suicide in the suicide-room. He will only answer to the suggestion of *felo de se* if this is already in him. To eradicate the tendency means the cultivation of a positive attitude of mind, together with a realisation that it is cowardice to try and escape from one's problems in this way—assuming it to be an escape. Exorcism, however—which, when all is said and done is simply a form of psychic disinfection exactly on a par with what is done in a physically dirty or contaminated house—may effectively clear up the bad psychic atmosphere of the room, so that there is less risk of latent depression or suicidal tendencies being roused into activity in those who go into it.

Obsession and Possession

Anyhow, the reassuring fact remains: that in any such case, whether of 'psychic' or of 'psychological' obsession or possession, man can learn to protect himself by the proper use of his own intrinsic powers. Exorcism or external psychological help are of value in their respective spheres; but the key to his difficulties lies in the will of the individual himself.

13

A SUMMING UP

To write intelligibly and reasonably about communication between two worlds must, of necessity, involve many apparent difficulties. On the one hand, one has to consider those so-called non-psychic observers, who study the subject on strictly intellectual lines. Even when they admit the genuineness of the psychic happenings, they regard them for the most part more as exhibitions of a strange abnormality than as the outward symbols of a curiously sensitive part of the human mechanism. On the other hand there are a great number of psychic people and unscientific experimenters who have put their experiences on record, giving them a highly emotional character.

Obviously, for any real understanding of this part of the field of human experience, some midway position must be found. A philosophy is needed which will satisfy the scientific mind by explaining logically the mechanism of the psychic person and the rationale of his work. It must also give due consideration to the underlying life element which is woven through all true experience, and which will not be confined in formula or set shape.

A Summing Up

The psychic has always a strong personal link with his work, being closely identified with it. Whether that psychic be a private person or a professional medium, he usually abhors any analysis. Hence, it has not so far been an easy task to bring together in friendly co-operation those methods of approach which lie along the opposite avenues of science and of personal experience. Thus, the reader who has had the patience to get this far may feel that the foregoing chapters are full of suggestions, but that they give no firm and definite answers. This is true. What is more, it is intentional, for the very reason that in matters such as we have considered there can be no final word. In every case, whether of haunting, mediumship, or other phenomenon suggesting contact between the psychic and the physical worlds, there are a number of possible explanations, and it is these we have aimed at suggesting, leaving it to the judgment of those present to try and discover the one most likely to apply to any specific instance. Each case needs to be judged on its own merits.

One idea at least seems original, which is that it is possible that the dead have a point of view of their own, which needs to be considered as seriously as the point of view of those who are in the body. Moreover, since we, in the flesh, function also at the psychic level where the dead are to be found, it seems that at that level we may be in contact with them quite as much as when they were alive. It is only in the flesh that we are blind to their presence: we miss them, but *do they miss us?* May we not, because of our fret and worry about them, make undue demand for their attention? For all we know, we may be as much of a nuisance to them at their level as a troublesome child can be to an adult who has his own business to attend to. It is at least a point worth thinking about.

A Summing Up

Some may feel that we have taken the whole question too much for granted. Others will feel that we are much too critical and destructive. Actually, we are at once sceptics and believers, both in matters of life in general and psychism in particular. For while, in something of a Kantian mood, we accept the general principles underlying many curious phenomena as a whole, we are always inclined to be doubtful of individual cases, and particularly of any glib interpretation of their origin and significance. It is, perhaps, for that very reason, that we are at once open-minded and doubters, that we are willing to leave to others the exposure of trickery or fraud. We ourselves are more concerned with considering how, on what general principle a certain phenomenon is likely to have been produced.

This attitude is in sharp contrast to that of the orthodox parapsychologist or psychical researcher. Yet if it was not for the work of these, our own attitude could not be justified. It is only the careful exposure of false claims which has proved to us beyond reasonable doubt that psychic phenomena can and do take place. We feel therefore that we can allow ourselves some elasticity where single cases are concerned. It is the principle which matters to us, the possible explanations of how phenomena may take place, rather than whether they are proved genuine in any special instance.

The contrast between the two attitudes is well illustrated by an occurrence when one of the writers was lecturing to a body of psychologists. He related an incident where an uneducated charwoman was speaking, while in trance, what was eventually proved to be archaic Persian. At question time he was asked how this was to be explained. He answered that the medium herself did not believe that her control was an outside entity, but that her *alter ego* was remembering things from a previous life.

'Well, maybe,' was his conclusion, and he was content to leave it at that, though had he gone further he would have elaborated other possibilities.

At that point, however, a distinguished parapsychologist in the audience got up and told of a similar case, the language being Latin, and how careful scrutiny went on to show that the medium, also an uneducated servant girl, had at one time worked in the house of a scholar who walked up and down his room declaiming Latin verse: she had obviously picked it up unconsciously and reproduced it in trance.

The first speaker was not in the least upset by this, because he was quite prepared to accept the same possibility in his case as an alternative to the tentative explanation put forward, both of them being equally likely; and there were still further possibilities. It did not matter, from the point of view of *principle*, that the Persian-speaking medium's past had not been gone into, even though it would matter a great deal if one were after isolated *facts*.

It is evident, therefore, that the reader has to be left in a most ambiguous position. Unless he is stimulated by it to try and make his own judgments, he may feel that he has been cheated, in the sense that what he thought he had has been taken away, and nothing given him in exchange. What is far more important than answering his questions, however, is to suggest how he can begin to discover satisfactory answers for himself.

Human beings can be divided into three main types, according to their reaction to new ideas. The first, probably

A Summing Up

the majority, are those who are uninterested. They are concerned simply with daily life at the material level, and ideas and abstractions affect them little more than they do the birds or the beasts. Then comes an intermediate type, those who have abstract ideas, but who like them cut, dried, and fixed. To them anything new is an annoyance or a cause for anxiety, and they automatically turn away from it, because mental and emotional comfort is more important to them than truth.

The third, and rarest, consists of people who ask for truth at all costs. They are willing, even if it should not always be easy, to let themselves doubt, to accept a challenge to cherished illusions; and, when they see good reason for it, they are willing to change their views. 'Consistency is the hobgoblin of little minds'; and, provided the inconsistency represents steady progress and not just grasshopper jumps to this and that unrelated point, it is accepted as an ineluctable necessity of life.

The first order will probably not read this book at all. The second will probably dislike it, because their minds and views are already made up. The third type may reject the views put forward if they seem to be distorted or untrue, but they will at any rate consider them before they do so.

To the middle class there is, however, one thing to say. It is axiomatic that life, and together with it mental development, must move forward. To all of us there come times of disturbance which precede a change of attitude, if we are to go on living and not merely existing. This is true about life in general and about doctrines and articles of faith in particular. But until we are ready, or getting ready, for such a change, we shall not be disturbed or upset by anything which suggests the need for a reassessment of values. In the development of science, the atomic theory was good enough until the scientific mind was prepared for a further step forward, when it passed into the world of electrons. This, in turn, led ultimately to further stages which have taken us to where we are now. But a pause between each forward move was as necessary as the forward movement itself when the time was ripe.

Hence, two considerations emerge. One is that there is virtue in beliefs which are only partially true; the other, that it is the reverse of virtue to cling to those beliefs when they are outgrown. In the subject of communication with other worlds, it is a step forward to discard the superstition which had smothered religion and to become a scientific materialist. But moving on from there, successive stages lead one on to a realisation that materialism is insufficient, and that man is certainly something more than his mortal body. Then we learn that the dead probably keep their human quality even after they have left the body, and are neither snatched away from us to some remote heaven, nor transformed into spiritual beings startlingly unlike the people we knew and loved as much for their frailties as for their transcendental qualities. Then the conception of continuous contact between those on either side of the veil again widens our view, while the realisation how much illusion may spoil that contact can only be taken as yet another advance. These are continuous and natural stages.

Nobody, whether a child or an adult, should have problems forced on him with which he is incapable of coping. If this happens, the result is collapse and breakdown. Hence, if a person is at the nursery-school stage of belief and experience, that belief is valuable to him and he should not be disturbed in it. But if he is ready to pass from the nursery to the kindergarten, he is equally in danger if he refuses to move on, and tries to be a spiritual Peter Pan.

Where beliefs are concerned, therefore, there is a mean course to be adopted. A senior student can do harm and upset a junior by forcing him on, or pressing him to accept views he is not yet ready to receive. But he can also do harm if he keeps to himself the knowledge he has acquired and does not give others the opportunity of sharing it. We must, however, wait until it is asked for, directly or tacitly. Moreover, since we are all in the junior school where life is concerned, everybody is likely to go astray and ride a personal hobby horse of the mind too far, unless he allows his fellows the chance of comparing their experience with his.

Therefore, if a new view of a subject upsets us, it is a good idea to take stock of ourselves and discover what it is we are reacting against. A shaky view of one's own can be disturbed, but not one that is true to us from real inner conviction. This is as true of psychic communications as of anything else. These should not be accepted too easily as being what they are supposed to be. But if the suggestion that they are not, is one which we are inclined to resent, it becomes necessary for us to find out whether this resentment is not due to our having received a mental challenge which we are reluctant to meet. It may be this, or it may be that the new idea is simply untrue to us. But if we have considered it objectively, then we will probably not feel resentment, but discard it quite dispassionately.

Emotional reaction is thus no criterion from which to work. Emotion is an irrational thing, though it follows valid laws of its own. But is reason itself enough? In theory it should be so, and logical argument, proceeding step by step from first premises to final conclusion, should

A Summing Up

be a sufficient standard by which to find truth. But in practice logical argument does not work, because of the limitation of the mind which conducts it. The intellect is essentially fallible because it is finite. It thinks sequentially, that is, it works within the framework of time and space. It is subject to the limitations of the space-time world; it perceives things only in parts, not as a whole.

The logical process is akin to watching a cinematograph film unfolding itself: one 'frame' follows another so quickly that to the eye the picture is a continuous, moving and sequential whole. Yet, actually, it proceeds in a series of jumps. And by means of a suitable technique, the logical development of an action can be led off imperceptibly into illusions and mysterious transformations which can be delightful to observe, by virtue of the very fact that they are indeed illusory and unrealistic, which is to say 'illogical'. But the delight and the sequence can only be assessed by a function of the mind which realises the film as a whole, not as a series of consecutive—or logical—steps, but by an instant response to the element of life in it. This synthetic quality is something beyond pure reason: it extends backward and forward in time, and allows us to conceive of things as wholes: it abstracts all the partial views given us of objects in the time world, and builds them into a unit which we can then look at as if it were before us, complete, at the immediate moment when we behold it.

That is the first step towards making a true assessment of a thing. We may from that viewpoint, look, so to speak, 'downward' to the time-world and see if it conforms to the steps of logic and reason. But this is still not enough. Something more is required before we should accept it as

A Summing Up

valid. In this we intuitively look 'up' or, perhaps, inward and apply what we have found to a purely individual touchstone to see if this particular idea is true *to us*. We have a phrase about something 'ringing a bell' in us. This is usually applied to memories, but it also very aptly describes the effect of a positive judgment made, not from outer comparisons, but from some subtle standard inside ourselves. We may be presented with a point of view which we do not understand, yet something in us leaps to it and makes us feel 'there is something true here'. On the other hand, we may see a much-praised picture, read a reputedly first-rate book, and yet, though we may appreciate the skill, artistic technique, or topicality which are in them, something tells us that the work is not quite sincere, or is somehow hollow or distorted.

It may be difficult to justify in reasonable terms a judgment made on such a basis, but to ourselves it is valid. We can say, at such times, 'I know'. Yet in that certainty there is also an intellectual element which says, 'I don't know, I am not absolutely sure'. For new knowledge is often both true and untrue. A communication from the dead may indeed be genuine, but the manner of its transmission can be an illusion. It is one of those paradoxical things when contradiction does not matter.

What does matter is that we should go on with our search for truth no matter how often we may deceive ourselves. It does not matter if other people disagree with us or do not believe us. We are not upset because they see things otherwise, and we have no emotional urge to impress on them what we know nor to convert them to our point of view. This is a very different attitude from that of the person with a mind set in a fixed pattern, whether of belief or incredulity.

A Summing Up

This is the only way in which to obtain an elastic hold on reality. It may be summarised thus:

'I know that this is true to me at the present moment. I know also that, as I learn more, this truth will change. My mind is a finite, limited thing, and can only show me one aspect of reality at a time. But what I have learned is that there is indeed a reality which is inalienable, indestructible, and eternal, but also inexpressible. In that, and that alone, I have absolute belief. Logic and reason can lead me towards that reality. They can also lead me away from it, by preventing me from considering imponderables. They are thus dangerous guides if I allow them to master me, but they are useful servants if I, the spiritual learner and knower, use them and direct them. I, the knower, am beyond both reason and unreason, beyond logic and that which cuts through logic. I, the knower, am the only one who is in a position to judge accurately of anything in heaven or earth.'

In short we may say without arrogance that we ourselves, ordinary human beings, have the power to find out all the secrets of the universe by slow process and in due season. The limited, time-dwelling aspects of our minds put obstacles between ourselves and reality. In so doing they shield us from the impact of the naked truth which—as in the case of St. Paul on the road to Damascus —would be too much for our immature personalities. If we want to find that truth, all that we need to do is to move the obstacles, to take down the shutters and roll up the blinds, when we shall find that the sun is there waiting for us to let it in and dispel the shadows of our ignorance.

There is, in fact, only one difficulty, and that is that the shutters are apt to stick and to resist our efforts to open them, while the blinds will not roll up without much work and effort. But one thing is certain. If it is Truth we are seeking, Truth we shall inevitably find in the end, long and arduous though we may make the way to it—for it is we who make the difficulties on that way; they are not of the way itself. Both the living and the dead can find that truth. There is little doubt that a closer co-operation exists between the two than most of us are aware of, or think possible. This contact, properly used and maintained by the communication of mind with mind and heart with heart—whether between those in the flesh or out of it—is one of the surest ways to it. But for this a positive attitude, and not the negative intervention of mediums is required.

The positive psychic as defined by us is a person who has done more than develop or make conscious an extra sense. He must have acquired some degree of wisdom, and have direct experience of reality. This shows him that there is a better way of extending his knowledge of life than by scurrying from place to place in search of experience at second-hand. He will look at things for himself, and accept as valid only that which he himself knows to be true, either because he has undergone it personally, or, because what he learns from others strikes up a note and taps some level of himself where true know-ledge is no longer personal but vicarious and available to all who can function at that level. It does not matter what name we give to it: universal mind, cosmic con-sciousness, illumination or the spiritual vision. It is the level of direct contact. And at that level he will know that people, whether living or dead, and objects, thoughts or feelings, whether concealed or accessible at the material level, are always within his reach. So to him there is no such thing as death nor painful separation. There is only change and progression, and that along the orderly lines of a plan formulated by some Intelligence beyond his understanding. He is thus brought back to a religious attitude: that of the only religion worth-while, which is the sense of order and mystery and of wonder, which grows unceasingly as his wisdom grows.

Hilversum (Holland),
Chelsea, London,
1948–9.

INDEX

Index